PENGU...
THE PENGUIN BOOK OF CLA...
AND ...

Ruskin Bond was born in Kasa...
and grew up in Jamnagar (Guj... the course of a writing career spanning forty years, he has written over a hundred short stories, essays, novels and more than thirty books for children. Three collections of short stories, *The Night Train at Deoli, Time Stops at Shamli* and *Our Trees Still Grow in Dehra* have been published by Penguin India. He has also edited two anthologies, *The Penguin Book of Indian Ghost Stories* and *The Penguin Book of Indian Railway Stories*.

The Room on the Roof was his first novel, written when he was seventeen, and it received the John Llewellyn Rhys Memorial Prize in 1957. *Vagrants in the Valley* was also written in his teens and picks up from where *The Room on the Roof* leaves off. These two novellas were published in one volume by Penguin India in 1993 as was a much-acclaimed collection of his non-fiction writing, *Rain in the Mountains. Delhi is not Far: The Best of Ruskin Bond* was published by Penguin India the following year.

Ruskin Bond received the Sahitya Akademi Award for English writing in India for 1992, for *Our Trees Still Grow in Dehra*.

The Penguin Book of Classical Indian Love Stories and Lyrics

Edited by Ruskin Bond

PENGUIN BOOKS

Penguin Books India (P) Ltd., 210, Chiranjiv Tower, 43, Nehru Place, New Delhi 110 019, India
Penguin Books Ltd., 27 Wrights Lane, London W8 5TZ, UK
Penguin Books USA Inc., 375 Hudson Street, New York, NY 10014, USA
Penguin Books Australia Ltd., Ringwood, Victoria, Australia
Penguin Books Canada Ltd., 10 Alcorn Avenue, Suite 300, Toronto, Ontario M4V 3B2, Canada
Penguin Books (NZ) Ltd., 182-190 Wairau Road, Auckland 10, New Zealand

First published by Penguin Books India (P) Ltd. 1996

Typeset in New Century Schoolbook by Digital Technologies and Printing Solutions, New Delhi

The photograph on page ix is from Ruskin Bond's collection of old postcards.

Kashmiri Song

Pale hands I loved beside the Shalimar,
    Where are you now? Who lies beneath your spell?
Whom do you lead on Rapture's roadway, far,
    Before you agonize them in farewell?
Oh, pale dispensers of my Joys and Pains.
    Holding the doors of Heaven and of Hell,
How the hot blood rushed wildly through the veins
    Beneath your touch, until you waved farewell.
Pale hands, pink-tipped, like lotus buds that float
    On these cool waters where we used to dwell,
I would rather have felt you round my throat
    Crushing out life, than waving me farewell!

—Lawrence Hope, *Songs from the Garden of Kama*

Contents

❧

The Penguin Book of Classical Indian
Love Stories and Lyrics

Introduction

❧

Kamadeva's arrows of love were made of flowers. His divine commander was *vasanta* (spring), who brought the trees and flowers into blossom and softened all creation for the sweet, irresistible attack of the god of love.

This nature-god is most in tune with India's Classical Age (roughly, the first thousand years AD), a time when the land was dominated by forests teeming with bird and animal life, and the human population was comparatively small and scattered. Countless kingdoms, large and small, made up the rich bejewelled pattern of India. Around the king's palace or fort grew small towns and bazaars and caravanserais for travellers, but just outside the city gates there was considerable verdure, with areas of cultivation fringing the great forests. This was a fit setting for the great legends and romances of gods and heroes and heroines. The *Ramayana* and the *Mahabharata* belonged to the earlier, Epic Age, but they provided stories that continued to be told and retold, culminating in Kalidasa's great verse-drama, *Shakuntala*, written in the early years of the new millennium. The great achievement of *Shakuntala* is in part due to its creator's love of nature. He is at his best in the lyrical passages describing the flora and fauna of the land. Shakuntala herself is half bird, her name being derived from the *shakuntas* or birds with which she held such easy converse.

Shakuntala is romantic and escapist, but this is not always the case with other writings of the period. The Classical Age saw the flourishing of the Sanskrit language, with an outpouring of poetry and drama. And Kamadeva was no chubby, infant Cupid. He was a mischievous, dexterous, youthful deity. His presence, visible or invisible, is felt in almost every story, love poem or prose work.

The literature of love and the literature of love-making are different. In the stories, poems and extracts presented here we find passion, desire, tenderness, jealousy, sensuality, even platonic love. But the art of love-making, described so inexhaustibly (exhaustingly?) in Vatsayana's *Kamasutra* (fourth century AD) does not really fall in the purview of this collection. It is not so much a story as a manual of sexual prowess. And it is easily available everywhere in many handsome editions.

In making this selection, I was looking for love literature that was not too well-known but which, nevertheless, was of high quality. Naturally I drew upon legend and folklore, of which there is a fair sampling; upon recent translations of classical Sanskrit, Tamil and Kannada literature; upon retellings from the epics; and upon some of the formative literature of the last century. Even then, I felt that something was missing—some tantalizing fragment, forgotten, neglected, unknown to me (and probably to the general reader) and which in some way sought to draw attention to itself.

Can a book draw attention to itself? Can an author reach out across the centuries, tap you on the shoulder, and say, 'Don't forget me. I, too, had something to say on the subject.' The idea is fanciful. Scholars search and discover, but I'm no scholar, I wait for the lucky find.

And as luck would have it—or perhaps the mischievous

Kamadeva, who has often numbered me among his victims, came to my rescue—I chanced upon a copy of E. Powys Mathers' English version (1927) of the *Kuttanimayam* of Damodaragupta, and the love poems of two Sanskrit poets, Amaru and Mayura, also translated by Mathers.

The story 'The Loves of Haralata and Sundarasena' is taken from Damodaragupta's little-known work, written in the eighth century AD. Nothing seems to be known of the author; and this appears to be but a fragment of his output. It is based on Louis de Langle's French translation.

When this story was written, we are told, the condition of the wife was negligible. She passed, at a far too early age, from the authority of the mother to that of her mother-in-law. She was despised if she remained childless; and, if she became a widow, she was not expected to survive her widowing.

The courtesan could only benefit from the wife's lack of independence. Her liberty was apparently protected by law; she could give or refuse herself. She was often able to obtain an education denied to the wife, and this education was both an attraction and a protection. She became more and more the ideal—'the one for whom to commit immortal follies'.

And yet, wrote Louis de Langle, 'Being at once both sensual and a mystic, the Hindu always asked too much of every luxurious circumstance, an agitation of passion . . . . he also expected sincerity and love. His too intense desire overleapt its object, and then reason proclaimed that object to be illusion.'

I think this helps us to know a little more about Damodaragupta's thinking, and to reconcile his savage bitterness with the tenderness running through his story.

Amaru was held in great esteem as a poet of the phases of love: desire and attainment, estrangement and reconciliation, joy and sorrow. He was one of the supreme early lyric poets of India. He lived around AD 800. There is a legend that Amaru was the hundred and first reincarnation of a soul which had previously occupied a hundred women. From a reading of his poems we can see how this legend might have arisen!

Mayura, who flourished in the first half of the seventh century, was a favourite of King Harsha (AD 606-647), but only a few erotic fragments of his work remain. The poems of Amaru and Mayura come from the Powys Mathers volume on 'Eastern Love'.

To turn to other works that add lustre to this collection, the recent translation by T.R.S. Sharma of Janna's Kannada classic, *Tale of the Glory-Bearer*, is represented by an extract which tells the story of the unfaithful queen who had an affair with a mahout, reputed to be the ugliest man in the kingdom. Physical deformities pale into insignificance when the chemistry between two people is just right!

Janna was a Jain poet of the twelfth and thirteenth century AD. He was the chief court poet of the Hoysala King, Veeraballala. Versions of this story are also found in Sanskrit, Hindi, Gujarati and Tamil.

The Tamil classic, *Shilappadikaram* (*The Ankle Bracelet*) by Prince Ilango Adigal, in the translation by Alain Danielou, is evocative in its descriptions of life in ancient India. The author was a Jain prince of the third century. Included in this selection is an extract from his verse epic in which he tells the story of young Kovalan who leaves his loyal wife Kannaki for the courtesan Madhavi. But the law of karma governs our lives, and Kovalam dies as a result of his infidelity.

Somadeva's *Kathasaritsagar* is a treasure-trove of stories, as its title 'Ocean of Stories' suggests. Worldly pleasure and power are the principal themes of this work. Arshia Sattar's recent translation from the Sanskrit provides the story 'The Courtesan Who Fell in Love'.

In going through some nineteenth century retellings of

legend and folklore, I have made selections from *The Indian Antiquary* which was edited in the 1880s and 1890s by Lt. Col. Sir Richard Temple. This learned journal brought together some wonderful tales from Punjab, Kashmir, Bengal, Gujarat, and other parts of western, central and southern India. Contributors to these now rare volumes included Flora Annie Steel, Putlibai Wadia, and G.H. Damant. Damant was a Deputy Commissioner of the Naga Hills who fell victim to the rebel Mozema Nagas during an uprising of that tribe in October 1879. Flora Annie Steel married a member of the Indian Civil Service and came to India in 1868. Her best known novel was *On the Face of the Waters* (1896), a balanced study of the 1857 uprising. Her *Tales from the Punjab* (1894) was a unique collection of retellings of oral legends.

Another civil servant who interested himself in Indian history and folklore was C.A. Kincaid. His many books included *Deccan Nursery Tales* and *A History of the Maratha People*. In his *Tales of Old Ind* he retold many of the romantic love stories of Sindh, Rajasthan, Gujarat and Punjab. Of the stories presented here, 'Momul and Rano' and 'Umar and Marai' are Sindhi in origin. 'Hir and Ranjho' and 'Suhni and Mehar' come from the Punjab.

In 1920, Shovana Devi (all I have is her name) brought out a little volume called *Tales of the Gods*, which gives us brief but charming renderings of some of the well-known tales from the epics, including the Shakuntala legend. (Kalidasa's verse drama is too long for inclusion here, and an extract would not have done justice to this seven-act play. But included is this great Sanskrit poet's other famous work, *Meghadutam (The Cloud-Messenger)* in the translation by Chandra Rajan. A lover-beloved relationship is implied between the earth and her cloud-lover, and the world-sustaining cloud also acts as a foil to the poem's hero, the passionate, love-sick yaksha.

Ruskin Bond

Meghadutam

Kalidasa

1

A certain yaksha unmindful of his appointed duties
and cursed by his lord to endure
a year's grievous separation from his beloved
dwelt exiled, his lustre dimmed, on Rama's hill
in hermitages thick with shade-trees and waters
hallowed by the touch of Janaka's daughter.

2

The impassioned lover having passed some months
on that hill, parted from her unsupported
—the golden armlet slipping down
to lay bare his wasted fore-arm—
saw on Asadha's most auspicious day
a cloud embracing the crest of the hill,
strikingly-shaped like a sportive elephant
bent down to butt a river bank.

'Meghadutam', from *The Loom of Time: A Selection of Kalidasa's Plays and Poems*, translated by Chandra Rajan. New Delhi: Penguin Books, 1989. The original Penguin edition carried diacritical marks. These have been dispensed with in this edition for the purpose of standardization.

3

Gazing on that which stirs the ketaka to bloom
the vassal lord of the King of Kings
brooded long,
with effort restraining his tears.
The sight of rain clouds makes even happy hearts
stir with restlessness;
what then of one far from her who longs
to hold him in close embrace.

4

With the month of rains approaching,
desiring to sustain his beloved's life,
hoping to send glad tidings of his well-being
through the life-giving cloud, he made with reverence
an offering of fresh blossoms of wild jasmine,
prefacing it with words of affection
and joyously welcomed the cloud.

5

Blended of mists and light, winds and water
can a mere cloud bear messages
that only the living with keen senses
and intelligence can convey?
Unmindful of this the yaksa entreated it,
overwhelmed by unreasoning eagerness;
indeed, the love-sick, their minds clouded,
confuse the sentient with the insentient.

6

Born in the lofty lineage of swirling diluvial clouds.
I know you are the god of thunder's minister
assuming what shape you will; so banished
from wife and kinsmen by divine decree, I entreat you
for it is nobler to address barren pleas

to the virtuous than fruitful to the vile.

7

You are the refuge. O Rain-Giver
for all who burn with anguish; so bear
a message from me parted from my love
by the wrath of the Lord of Treasures;
go then to Alaka, abode of the Yaksha Lord,
her palaces washed by moonlight
streaming from Shiva's brow
where He is seated in her outer groves.

8

Women whose husbands travel to far lands,
pushing back their straggling hair
will eagerly look up to see you
riding high on the path of the wind,
and draw comfort; for when you arrive
all clad and girt for action,
who can ignore his lonely wife distraught
unless subject like me to an alien will?

9

While a friendly breeze impels you gently
as you loiter along, and here on your left
the cataka in its pride sings sweetly,
hen-cranes will know the time ripe for mating
and rejoice when they note in the sky
your eye-delighting presence; rest assured
they will attend on you in patterned flight.

10

Arriving there unimpeded you are certain
to see that constant lady,
your brother's wife still living
engrossed only in counting the days;

Hope's slender thread serves to hold
the flower-hearts of women
tender and prone to droop too soon
under the burden of separation.

11

And, hearing your thunder—a sound sweet to their
ears—
that can make Earth unfurl her mushroom parasols,
regal swans longing for Manasa-lake,
gathering tender lotus-shoots for the way
will be your companions in the sky
even up to Mount Kailasa's peak.

12

Embrace and bid farewell to your loving friend,
this lofty mountain girdled by slopes marked
by the holy feet of the Lord of Raghus
adored by the world,
Time and again, reuniting with you,
it displays its affection, breathing out
burning sighs born of long separation.

13

Listen first, while I describe the way
fitting for your journey which you will follow
resting your foot on mountains when weary,
refreshed when wasted by the clear water of streams:
then you shall hear my message, O Rain-Giver,
drinking it in eagerly with your ears.

14

While simple Siddha maidens with upturned faces,
watching your impetuous power tremble in alarm
and cry: 'Is the wind carrying off the mountain's peak?'

soar high up into the sky facing north,
far above this thicket of sap-filled nicula,
shunning on your path the proud sweep of the heavy
trunks
of the elephants that guard the sky's quarters.

15

Here to the east, a fragment of Indra's bow
springs spectacular from the hill top, gleaming
as if blended of the lustres of brilliant gems.
Shot through by its sheen, your dark-blue body
shines resplendent like Vishnu's in his cowherd guise,
lit up by irridescent peacock-plumes.

16

While rustic women unversed in eyebrow play
drink you in with eyes moist with happiness
knowing the harvest to depend on you,
ascend the upland plains fragrant from fresh furrowing;
then veering slightly to the west, speed on
keeping ever to the north.

17

As you approach the noble mountain Citrakuta,
he will greet you, O travel-weary Rain-Giver,
and bear you on his head held high: you too
with sharp showers will quench summer's cruel fires.
The tenderness of true feeling in the great
bears fruit in no time, returning kindness for kindness.

18

With his forest fires fully quenched by your sharp
showers,
Amrakuta will bear you gratefully
on his crown, travel-weary as you are;

even the meanest remembering former favours
will not turn his face away from a friend
who seeks shelter; what then of one so lofty!

19

Its slopes all aglow with the ripened fruit
of wild mangoes, and you on its peak set
like a coil of dark glossy hair, the mountain
—seeming Earth's breast—dark-blue centre
encircled by pale-gold expansive curves—
will appear entrancing to celestial lovers.

20

Resting awhile on that mountain
in whose bowers the brides of foresters sport,
and lightened by your waters' outpouring
you'll speedily cross the road beyond
and see Reva's streams spreading dishevelled
at Vindhya's uneven rocky foothills,
inlaying them like ashen streaks
decorating an elephant's body.

21

Your rain disgorged, draw up that river's water
whose flow impeded by rose-apple brakes
is pungent with the scent of wild elephants in rut,
and journey on; gaining inner strength
the wind cannot make light of you, O Rain-Cloud;
for hollowness makes things light; fullness bestows
weight.

22

Seeing the green-gold Nipa flowers
with their stamens half-emerging
and the Kandal is showing their early buds
along the edge of every pool,

savouring the rich fragrance of the earth
in the forests burnt by fire,
antelopes will chart your path as you pass
shedding fresh rain drops.

23

Siddhas watching catakas
skilled catching falling rain drops,
and pointing out to egrets in flight,
counting them on their fingers,
will pay you their grateful respect,
suddenly obtaining a flurry of unexpected embraces
from their beloved wives clinging to them in alarm
trembling at the sound of your thunder.

24

Even though you would wish to proceed with speed
for the sake of my happiness, my friend,
I foresee delay while you loiter
on peak after peak fragrant with wild jasmine;
ough peacocks, their eyes moist with joy may greet you
ith welcoming cries, I pray you, try to hasten onward.

25

The Dasarnas will put on a new beauty
at your approach:
woodland ringed round by ketakas
with needle-pointed buds newly-opened
will glow a pale gold:
birds starting to nest will throng
the sacred peepuls in the village squares:
rose-apple groves will darken
with the sheen of ripening blue-black fruit
and wild geese settle for a few days.

26

When you reach that royal city, Vidisa by name
widely renowned, you shall at once obtain
the unalloyed fulfilment of a lover's desire,
tasting Vetravati's sweet waters as a lover his beloved's
lips,
with sonorous thunder passing along her banks
as she flows with knitted brows of tremulous wavelets.

27

There you shall alight seeking rest on Nicai hill
thrilling with delight at your touch
as Kadambas burst into sudden bloom;
the hill loudly proclaims through grottoes
exhaling fragrances of pleasure,
passions unrestrained of the city's youth
dallying there in love-sports with courtesans.

28

Having rested, go on, sprinkling with fresh rain drops
clusters of jasmine-buds in gardens by woodland streams,
enjoying a fleeting together-ness
as your gift of shade touches
the faces of flower-gathering maidens, who
each time they wipe the sweat off their cheeks, bruise
the wilting lotuses hung at their ears.

29

As your course points due north to Alaka,
the way to Ujjayini is a detour no doubt,
but do not therefore turn away from a visit to her
palace-terraces.
Indeed you would have lived in vain if you do not dally
there
with the tremulous eyes of the city's beautiful women
that dart in alarm at the branched lightning's flashes.

30

On your path, when you meet Nirvindhya
wearing a girdle strung of chiming bells
—a row of water-birds plashing on her undulating
waves—
weaving her sinuous course with charming unsteady gait
to reveal eddies forming her navel
—such coy gestures are women's first statements of
love—
be sure to be filled with love's fine flavour.

31

Crossing that river, O fortunate lover,
yours will be the happy task to induce Sindhu
visibly grieving at your absence,
her waters shrunk to a thin braid and pale
with the paleness of dry leaves
fallen from trees rooted on her banks,
to cast off the sorrow withering her.

32

Reaching Avanti whose village-elders
are well-versed in the Udayana-tales,
go towards that city already spoken of;
to Ujjayini glowing in splendour
like a brilliant piece of Paradise
come down to earth with traces of merits
of dwellers in Paradise returning,
the fruit of their good deeds almost spent.

33

At day-break in Ujjayini, Sipra's cool breeze
scented with the fragrance of lotuses comes
prolonging the piercing cries of love-maddened
saras-cranes.
Refreshing to the tired limbs of women

after passion's ecstatic play, it removes
their languor like an artful lover
plying his love with amorous entreaties.

34 & 35

Smoke drifting through lattice-screens
from aromatic gums that perfume women's hair
enhances your beautiful form;
Palace-peacocks out of fellow-feeling
present you their gift-offering of dance;
worn out with travel, having passed the night
in her flower-fragrant mansions marked with red lac
from the feet of lovely ladies, approach
the holy shrine of Candesvara, Preceptor of the
Triple-World,
watched with awe by the Lord's attendants,
because your hue is the blue of His throat.
Its gardens are stirred by Gandhavati's breezes
scented with the pollen of blue-lotuses
and fragrances wafted from unguents
used by young women sporting in her waters.

36

If by chance you reach Mahakala at a time other than
sunset,
stay on till the sun disappears from sight;
by performing the exalted office of the temple-drum
in the evening-rituals offered to the spear-armed Lord
you will enjoy the full fruit, O Rain-Bearer,
of the deep-throated rumblings of your thunder.

37

With jewelled belts tinkling as they move with measured
steps,
temple-dancers whose hands tire, gracefully waving
chowries with glittering gem-studded handles.

will taste from the first rain-drops you shed,
pleasure as from a lover's nail-marks and shower on you
sidelong glances streaming like a line of honey-bees.

38

Then bathed in evening's glow red as fresh china rose
flowers
when the Lord of Beings commences His Cosmic Dance,
encircling, merging into the forest of His uplifted arms,
dispel His desire to wear the blood-moist elephant-hide,
your devotion observed by Bhavani
with steady eyes, her terror now calmed.

39

Young women going to their lovers' dwellings at night
set out on the royal highway mantled
in sight-obscuring darkness you could pierce with a pin;
light their path with streaked lightning
glittering like gold-rays on a touchstone,
but do not startle them with thunder and pelting rain
for they are easily alarmed.

40

On the top most terrace of some turreted mansion
where ring-doves sleep,
pass the night with your lightning-wife
much-fatigued by continual play. But pray
resume your journey the moment the sun rises;
surely, those who undertake to help a friend
do not linger over providing that help.

41

Philandering husbands come home at sunrise
called on to comfort their anguished wives
by drying the welling tears of betrayal;
therefore move quickly out of the sun's path;

he too returns at dawn to the lotus-pool
to dry the dew-tears on her lotus-face;
he would be not a little incensed
that you obstruct his bright ray-fingers.

42

Your self intrinsically beautiful
even in its shadow-form will enter Gambhira's clear
waters
as into a tranquil pool of consciousness;
do not therefore cavalierly dismiss
her welcoming glances—those dazzling upward leaps
of glittering white fishes bright as water-lilies.

43

Her dark-blue waters like a garment
slipping off the sloping bank of her hips,
still cling to the reed-branches
as if lightly held up by one hand;
drawing it away as you bend over her, my friend,
will it not be hard for you to depart?
For who can bear to leave a woman, her loins bared,
once having tasted her body's sweetness?

44

Fragrant with the scent of the earth freshened by your
showers,
a cool wind that ripens the fruit on wild fig-trees
is inhaled with delight by elephants
through their water-spout-trunks;
it will waft you gently to the Lord's hill
that you seek to approach.

45

Skanda has made that hill his fixed abode;
transform yourself into a flower-cloud

and shower him with blossoms moist with Ganga's
      celestial waters;
   for he is the blazing energy, sun-surpassing,
   that the wearer of the crescent-moon placed
in the Divine Fire's mouth to protect Indra's hosts.

46

Then, let your thunder magnified by the echoing
      mountain
spur the peacock the fire-born god rides, to dance,
its eyes brightened by the radiance of Shiva's moon;
      Bhavani out of affection for her son
      places its fallen plume
gleaming with irridescent circlets on her ear
   in place of the lotus-petal she wears.

47

Having thus worshipped
   the god born in a thicket of reeds
   and travelling some distance
   as Siddha-couples bearing lutes
leave your path free, from fear of water-drops,
bend low to honour Rantideva's glory sprung
   from the sacrifice of Surabhi's daughters
   and flowing on earth changed into a river.

48

Stealing the colour of the god who draws the horn-bow
      as you bend down to drink its waters,
sky-rangers looking down will indeed see with wonder
      that river from the far distance
      as a thin line, broad though she is,
   as if Earth wore a single strand of pearls
      set with a large sapphire at the centre.

49

Crossing that river go onwards making
yourself the target for the eager eyes
of Dasapura's women accomplished
in the graceful play of curving eye-brows,
their eyes with upturned lashes flashing
with the beauty of gazelles leaping up
and far surpassing the grace of honey-bees
on white jasmines swaying.

50

Ranging with your shadow through the land
of Brahmavarta stretching below Kuru's field,
do not fail to visit the battleground
that marks the great war of the barons,
where the wielder of the Gandiva-bow
showered hundreds of sharp arrows on princely faces
as you shoot driving downpours on lotuses.

51

The Plough-Bearer, turning away from that war
out of affection for his kinsmen, renounced
the cherished wine reflecting Revati's eyes
and worshipped Sarasvati's waters; you too,
enjoying those waters, O gentle Sir,
will become pure within, dark only in form.

52

From there you should visit Jahnu's daughter
near Kanakhala's hill where she comes down
the slopes of the Lord of Mountains, making
a stairway for Sagara's sons going up to Heaven.
She grasped Shiva's matted hair
clinging with wave-hands to His crest-jewel, the moon,
foam-laughter mocking the frown on Gauri's face.

53

If you aim to drink her clear crystal waters slantwise,
hanging down by your hind-quarters in the sky
like some elephant out of Paradise,
as your shadow glides along her stream
she would appear beautiful at once as though
she and Yamuna flowed together at that spot.

54

Reaching that river's true birth-pace, the mountain
white with snows, its rocks scented by musk deer lying
there;
and reclining on its peak to remove
the long journey's weariness, you will wear
a beauty comparable to the stain on the horn
of the triple-eyed lord's white bull rooting in the mud.

55

If a forest-fire born of cedar branches
clashing in the blowing wind
should assail the mountain, and its fiery sparks
scorch the bushy tails of yaks,
pray quench it fully with a thousand sharp showers.
The riches of the great are best employed
to ease the miseries of the distressed.

56

Unable to bear the thunder hurled down,
Sarabhas on the mountain puffed up with pride
will suddenly spring up in fury towards you
who are beyond reach, only to shatter their own limbs;
scatter them with your tumultuous laughter of hail.
Who indeed that undertakes vain-glorious acts
would not become the butt of ridicule!

57

Bending low in adoration, go round
the rock bearing the foot-print of the moon-crested Lord,
perpetually worshipped with offerings by Siddhas;
looking upon it, the body abandoned
and sins shaken off, the faithful gain
the Eternal Station of the Lord's attendants.

58

The wind breathing through hollow bamboos makes
sweet music;
woodland nymphs sing with passion-filled voices
of the victory over the triple-city;
if your thunder rumbles in the glens like a drum
would not the ensemble then be complete
for the Dance-Drama of the Lord of Beings?

59

Passing over many marvels on Himalaya's slopes,
you should go north through the narrow Krauncá-pass
—gateway for wild geese and path to glory
for the Bhrigu Chief—lengthened out cross-wise,
beautiful like Vishnu's dark-blue foot
stretched out to curb Bali's pride.

60

Still climbing higher, be Kailasa's guest
—mirror for goddesses—the joints of its ridges
cracked by ten-faced Ravana's straining arms.
Towering up into the sky with lofty peaks
radiant like white water-lilies, it stands
as if it were the wild laughter
of the Parent of the Triple-World
piled up through the ages.

61

When, glistening like smooth-ground collyrium, you lean
    dark on its slopes white as ivory freshly cut,
that mountain, I imagine would, like the Plough-Bearer
    with a dark-blue mantle slung o'er his shoulder
      attain to a grace so arresting
      as to hold the gaze entranced.

62

And if Gauri should stroll on that mountain
    created for play, holding Shiva's hand
    divested of its snake-bracelet,
    hardening your mass of waters within,
    form yourself into wave-like steps
and go before her as she climbs the jewelled slopes.

63

When struck by swarms of sparks off Indra's thunderbolt
    your water-jets shoot out, celestial maidens there
    will surely use you for their bath;
    having found you in summer's heat, my friend,
    if these girls eager for play will not let you go,
you should scare them with harsh-sounding roars.

64

Sipping Manasa waters where golden lotuses grow,
    joyfully giving Airavata
    the fleeting pleasure of your veiling shade,
    fluttering with rain-drenched breezes
    the fine silk garments of tender leaves
    the Tree of Paradise wears,
    amuse yourself on that majestic mountain
whose jewelled slopes glitter in chequered light and
      shade.

65

Once seen, O wanderer-at-will, you cannot but recognize
Alaka on its upper slope seated as on her lover's lap
—Ganga, her fine garment, falling down—
High over her many-storied mansions
like a woman with her hair piled up
and bound in a net of pearls, she bears
masses of clouds shedding water in the rainy season.

66

Where palaces with their cloud-kissing tops
equal you in loftiness,
and their gem-paved floors rival the glitter
of your glistening rain drops;
where paintings on the walls vie
with your rainbow hues;
and graceful movements of lovely women
rival the lightning's play;
where drums beaten to the sound of music
resemble your thunder, mellow, deep-throated:
And in each particular more than compare with you.

67

Where women toy with a lotus held in the hand,
twine fresh jasmines in their hair;
the beauty of their faces glows pale gold
dusted with the pollen of Lodhra flowers;
fresh amaranth-blooms encircle the hair-knot,
a delicate Sirisa nestles at the ear;
and on the hair-parting lie Kadamba blossoms
born at your coming.

68

Where yakshas accompanied by highborn ladies
resort to their palace-terraces
paved with precious gems star-flower-mirroring,

to partake of passion-kindling flower wines
pressed from the Tree of Paradise,
while drumheads softly struck
throb deep-throated tones like yours.

69

Where at sunrise the path followed at night
by amorous women hastening to midnight trysts
with faltering steps, is marked by telltale signs—
Mandara flowers fallen from playful curls
and petals of golden lotuses worn at the ears,
dislodged, lie strewn on the ground, with pearls
scattered loose as the threads snapped
of bodices of pearls that closely held their breasts.

70

Where lovers undoing the knot at the waist, hands
trembling with passion,
toss aside silken garments loosening,
yaksha women with lips like Bimba fruit,
overcome by shy confusion
aim handfuls of aromatic powder
at glittering gems serving as lamps.
Ah! What fruitless throws even though they hit their
mark.

71

Where, led to terraces of lofty mansions
by their guide the ever-moving wind,
rain clouds like you stain the paintings
with droplets of water;
then, seeming fearful flee at once
fragmented through lattices,
assuming with practised skill
the shapes of smoke streaming out.

72

Where at midnight moonstones
hanging from networks of threads,
touched by the moon's feet
resplendent as you move away
shed clear drops of coolness
to dispel the languor born
of oft-enjoyed loveplay in women
just released from a loved husband's close embrace.

73

Where, knowing the Supreme One to dwell incarnate,
friend to the Lord of Treasures,
the God of Love out of fear refrains from drawing
his bow strung with honeybees,
his work accomplished by lovely women
displaying their alluring charms, who bend
the bow of their eyebrows to shoot bright glances
unerringly at Love's targets.

74

There, to the north of the palaces
of the Lord of Treasures stands our home
recognizable from afar by its arched gateway
beautiful as the rainbow.
Close by grows a young Mandara tree
nurtured by my love like a son and now bending
with clusters of blossoms
within reach of her hand.

75

A flight of steps, all emerald slabs—
a pool patterned over
by full-blown lotuses on glossy beryl stems—
Wild geese haunt its waters, freed from restless longing,
no longer resorting to nearby Manasa-lake

even after they see you coming.

76

By its edge is a miniature hill, wondrous,
with sapphire-inlaid crest, exquisitely blue
and ringed round by golden plantain-trees.
Watching you glitter at the edges with lightning-gleams
my heart trembles struck by the memory of that hill, my
friend,
remembering how dear it was to my beloved wife.

77

On it by a fragrant jasmine bower
encircled by a hedge of amaranth
stands a red Ashoka fluttering its tender leaves,
and the dearly-loved Kesara too.
One craves the touch of your friend's lovely foot,
the other longs for the wine of her mouth,
pretending it is blossom-time.

78

And between them a golden rod rising
from a pedestal of jade whose sheen
rivals that of bamboos newly-sprouted
supports a crystal tablet;
your blue-throated friend
settles on it at close of day
after my love clapping her hands has made him dance
to the sweet tinkling of her bracelets.

79

By these tokens of recognition
treasured in your heart, O wise one!
And noting the beautifully-drawn forms
of lotus and conch on the sides of the door,
you will know the mansion, its lustre dimmed

no doubt by my absence: when the sun has set
the lotus does not show forth in all its glory.

80

At once becoming small as an elephant cub
for a speedy descent, seated on the charming crest
of that pleasure-hill I described before,
you may easily dart into the mansion
faint lightning-glances twinkling
like a glittering line of fireflies.

81

There you will see her, in the springtime of youth,
slender,
her teeth jasmine-buds, her lips ripe bimba-fruit,
slim-waisted, with deep navel
and the tremulous eyes of a startled doe,
moving languidly from the weight of her hips,
her body bowed down a little by her breasts
—Ah! The Creator's master-work among women.

82

Know her to be my second life,
alone, speaking little,
mourning like a cakravaki
her companion far away.
With the passing of these long days, racked
by intense longing, the young girl
would appear so changed I think,
like a lotus-plant struck by the chilling hoar-frost.

83

Weeping passionately, her eyes would be swollen
and her lips withered by burning sighs;
my beloved's face cupped in the palm of her hand,
only glimpsed through loose tresses flowing down

would surely appear like the miserable moon
stricken pale when shadowed by you.

84

She will come into your view absorbed
in the day's rites of worship or drawing my likeness
imagined wasted by separation
or asking the melodious songster in the cage,
'sweet one, do you remember our lord?
You were a favourite with him.'

85

Or, clad in a drab garment she may place
the lute on her lap, wishing to sing a melody
set to words signifying my name;
succeeding somehow in tuning the strings
wet with her tears, O gentle friend, she forgets
again and again the sequence of notes
even though she composed it herself.

86

Or, beginning with the day of our parting
she may count the months remaining,
laying out in order on the floor,
flowers placed at the threshold;
or, savouring imagined pleasures of love
treasured in her heart:
—such are the only diversions of women
sorrowing in the absence of their husbands.

87

Occupied by day, the pangs of loneliness
would not distress your friend too keenly,
but I fear the nights devoid of diversions
would pass heavy with grief;
therefore, I pray, meet the faithful girl

at midnight with my messages,
standing at the window close to where she lies
wakeful on the ground, and comfort her.

88

Wasted by anguish
she would be lying on her bed of loneliness
drawing herself together on one side,
seeming like the last sliver
of the waning moon on the eastern horizon.
By my side her nights flew by
on winged moments in rapture's fullness;
now they drag on, heavy with her burning tears.

89

With a burning sigh that withers her lips
tender as leaf-buds, you will see her
toss aside those curling tresses
rough with frequent ritual-baths,
that stray down her cheeks uncared for.
Longing for sleep, hoping in dreams at least
she would be one with me in love,
a sudden torrent of tears might wash away those hopes.

90

On that first day of parting, her tresses
with their wreath of flowers stripped off were twisted
and plaited into one single braid
which I shall unwind when the curse is ended
and all my sorrows melted away:
you will see her with untrimmed nails pushing
that tangled braid, rough and painful to the touch,
repeatedly off the curve of her cheek.

91

Remembering past delights her eyes would turn

towards the moonbeams, cool, ambrosial,
streaming in through the lattices,
and turn away at once in sorrow.
Veiling her eyes with lashes heavy-laden with tears
she will seem to be hovering uncertain
between waking and dreaming
—a day-lily on a cloudy day neither open nor shut.

92

Casting aside all adornments,
keeping alive her fragile body in measureless sorrow,
desolate, my love would try in vain
time and again to throw herself on her bed;
the sight I am sure will make you shed some freshwater
tears;
for tender hearts ever melt in compassion.

93

I know well your friend's heart is filled with love for me,
hence I believe her brought to this pitiable state
in this our very first parting.
It is not vain self-esteem that makes a braggart of me;
all I have said, my brother,
you will soon see before your very eyes.

94

Lack-lustre without glossy collyrium,
the sidelong glance blocked by straying hair,
the eyebrow's graceful play forgotten
through abstaining from wine,
the doe-eyed lady's left eye
would throb at your coming, I guess,
and match the charm of blue lotuses
quivering as fishes dart among them.

95

And her left thigh—bare of my nail marks,
unadorned by the network of pearls of the long-worn zone
she cast aside struck by the turn of fate,
so used to the gentle stroking of my hands
after love's enjoyment—
pale as a tender plantain's stem will start quivering.

96

If at that time, O Rain-Giver,
she has found happiness, pray wait near her,
just one watch of the night withholding your thunder,
having striven hard to find me, her beloved,
in a dream of love, let not her arms
twined like tender vines round my neck in close embrace,
suddenly fall away from their hold.

97

Awakening her with a breeze
cooled by your fine spray, when revived
along with the fragrant jasmine's
fresh clusters of buds, she gazes intensely
at the casement graced by your presence,
begin to address the noble lady
in vibrant tones courteous,
with your lightning-gleams hidden deep within you.

98

O unwidowed lady! Know me,
your husband's dear friend, and rain cloud
come to tender to you
his messages treasured in my heart.
With deep but gentle tones
I speed weary travellers yearning
to unknot the tangled braids of their grieving wives,

on their way home from distant lands.

99

Thus addressed, like Mithila's princess
lifting her face up to the Son of the Wind,
she will gaze on you, her heart opening
like a flower from eager expectation:
welcoming you at once, with deep respect
she'll listen with rapt attention, gentle friend;
for news of husbands brought by a friend
are to women the closest thing to reunion.

100

O long-lived one! In response to my plea
and to honour yourself, speak to her thus:
your consort lives,
haunting Ramagiri's hermitages,—
parted from you he asks
if all is well with you, tender lady!
Such soothing words should be addressed first
to living beings who fall prey to calamity.

101

Far off, his way barred by adverse decree,
in his imaginings
his body becomes one with your body;
thin with thin,
anguished with intensely anguished,
tear-drowned with tear-drenched
yearning with endlessly yearning,
your hotly-sighing body
with his racked by long drawn-out sighs.

102

Who, before your companions
loved to whisper in your ear

what could well be said aloud indeed,
for he longed to touch your face,
he, gone beyond range of your hearing,
not seen by your eyes, speaks
through my mouth to you, these words
shaped by his intense yearning.

103

In the syama-vines I see your body,
your glance in the gazelle's startled eye,
the cool radiance of your face in the moon,
your tresses in the peacock's luxuriant train,
your eyebrow's graceful curve in the stream's small
waves;
but alas! O cruel one, I see not
your whole likeness anywhere in any one thing.

104

Scent of warm earth rain-sprinkled, rising fresh,
O my darling, as the fragrance of your mouth, and
the God of Love, five-arrowed, wastes my frame
already wasted, grieving, far from you.
For pity's sake, think how my days pass
now at summer's close, as massed rain clouds
rending the sunshine, scatter the pieces
and cling enamoured to the sky in all directions.

105

With bright ores, I draw you on a rock
feigning anger, but when I wish
to draw myself fallen at your feet,
at once my eyes are dimmed by ever-welling tears.
Ha! How cruel is fate that even here
it will not suffer our reunion.

106

Striving hard I find you in a waking dream,
I stretch my arms out into the empty air
to fold you in a passionate embrace.
Those large pearl-drops clustering on tender leaf-shoots
are surely—are they not—the tears
the tree-goddesses shed watching my grief?

107

Sudden, Himalayan breezes split open
the tightly-shut leaf-buds on deodars,
and redolent of their oozing resin
blow south; I embrace those breezes
fondly imagining they have of late
touched your limbs. O perfect one!

108

If only the long-drawn-out night
could be squeezed into a single moment,
if only the hot summer's day
would glow at all times with a gentle warmth;
my heart, breathing the unattainable prayers
is left a defence-less prey,
O lady with bright-glancing eyes!
To the fierce pangs of separation from you.

109

But no more of me; reflecting deeply
I bear up, drawing on my own inner strength;
you too, lady most blessed,
should resist falling into utter dejection.
Whom does happiness always attend
or misery always befall
Man's state on earth like the rim of a wheel
goes down and comes up again.

110

With Vishnu risen from His serpent couch
my curse shall be ended; closing your eyes
make the four remaining months go by;
then on autumnal night with moonlight
we two shall taste together every desire
eagerly imagined when we were apart.

111

And further he said this: once in bed
asleep, still clinging to my neck
you woke up on a sudden, weeping a little,
and when I asked why again and again,
laughing to yourself you said,
—ah, you cheat, I saw you in my dream
playing with another woman.

112

By this token of recognition
know that I am well; and do not doubt me
O dark-eyed one, believing idle reports
that say for no good reason
that absence destroys the affections;
Ah no, the lack of pleasure makes
the craving intense for what is desired,
piling it up into love's great hoard.

113

I trust, noble friend, you are resolved
to do this kindly service for me?
I cannot think your grave look forbodes refusal;
without a sound you offer catakas
the water they crave; the answer
noble ones make is to do the thing wished for.

114

Having granted this wish so dear to my heart,
strange as it may seem,
for friendship's sake or out of pity for me, desolated,
wander, O Cloud, in all the lands you choose,
gathering greater glory in the rains;
may you never be parted from the lightning
even for an instant.

The Approach of Spring

Prince Ilango Adigal

❦

Canto Eight

The Approach of Spring

The celebrated god of Love, with Spring, his gracious friend, ruled the fertile Tamil land that spread from the northern Venkata hills, where Vishnu the saviour of the world resides, to the southern virgin sea. The country had four capitals: Urandai the luxurious, Madurai of the high ramparts, Vanji the strong, and Puhar the guardian of the sea.

The approach of Spring was announced by its messenger, the south wind, blowing from green Mount Podiyil, that peak sanctified by the stay of Agastya, the sage all men respect. As if trumpeting the order—'Soldiers of the dragon prince, dress ranks!'—the cuckoo, bugler of the great army of Eros, sounded its shrill notes through the

'The Approach of Spring', from *Shilappadikaram* (The Ankle Bracelet) by Prince Ilango Adigal, translated by Alain Danielou. New Delhi: Penguin Books, 1993. The original Penguin edition carried diacritical marks. These have been dispensed with in this edition for the purpose of standardization.

dense forest, which a curtain of creepers made impenetrable.

After her break with Kovalan in the flowery pleasure grove by the sea, blossom-eyed Madhavi came back alone to her rich home, and climbed to her summer refuge, a tower near the sky. For her own pleasure, the elegant girl decked her heavy saffron-powdered breasts with pearls from the southern sea and sandal from the hills. Holding her faultless harp, she sang a tender melody that filled her heart with grief. Then, to forget, she sat in the lotus posture.

Her right hand on the harp's body took the flag position (*pataka*); her left hand lay resting on the instrument's neck (*madagam*). She was an expert in sounding various notes strongly (*arppu*), softly (*kudam*), or tenderly (*adirvu*), avoiding all dissonance. She played the fourteen notes of the classical scale, beginning with the fourth (*ulai*) in the lowest octave, and ending with the third (*kaikkilai*). She carefully searched for the exact pitch of each note, tuning the second (*inai*) on the fifth (*kilai*), the sixth (*valari*) on the third (*pakai*) and the fourth (*natpu*). She sang, using as drone the harp's fifth string (*ili*).

Then she sounded the fifth and seventh (*taram*), beginning and ending first on the fourth, later on the tonic (*kural*). She practiced the four groups of modes (*marudam*), the *ahanilai*, the *puranilai*, the sixteen-stringed *maruhiyal*, and the *peruhiyal* with its thiry-two notes. Careful of the three shades of pitch, high, median, and low, that may colour the notes, she played some graceful melodies (*tirappan*). Soon this flowering liana felt weary and started elegant variations (*venirpani*).

She then made a garland of champak, mixed with *madhavi, tamala,* jasmine, and fragrant roots, in hooked pandanus flowers. Taking a long bamboo stylus, she dipped it in a writing paste made of lacquer mixed with glue, and inscribed a message inspired in her by Eros, who, armed with his flowery shafts, was imposing his rule upon the world:

The Letter

Spring, the world's worst tyrant,
is an irresponsible lad
who hurls one on another
most ill-assorted lovelorn hearts.

Though not free of defect, the Moon
arises, kindling ardent wants
that evening soon makes unendurable.
Eros may well, in sport,
assail with deadly flower-darts
a few hearts that are lonely,
be they lovers that have parted, or
those waiting for a certain one's return,
or former lovers who have gone away,
the once dear cherished face forgot.
Please try to understand my pain.

Thus pale Madhavi, perfect in the sixty-four arts, wrote on the wreath, showing the naked depth of her passion. While she was carefully writing, she hummed, like a small child, a mode *(pan)* and its prelude *(tiram)*.

When the evening had brought her peace, she sent for Vasanta-mala, her handmaid, and bade her go to Kovalan, to repeat before him all the words inscribed on the wreath of flowers, and to bring him back to her arms. Vasanta-mala, who had long eyes like arrowheads, carried the garland to Kovalan's home near the grain merchants' residences. She herself placed it in his hands.

Kovalan refused the garland and murmured:

'A dancing girl in love once performed the prelude *(kankuduvari)*, with a red mark on her brow and flowers in her hair. Her thin eyebrows were dark; her eyes, resembling two water lilies, sent alluring glances. Her nose was like a *kumil* bud, her lips a *kovvai* flower.

'Then this girl with the long dark eyes showed us an inviting variation, the *kanvai,* coming forward but shyly withdrawing again, her moonlike face oppressed by the weight of her hair, heavier than the rain clouds. Her eyes were like quivering carps, and her enticing smile showed the pearls of her teeth set in the coral of her lips.

'She next revealed a character-dance *(ulvari).* Her piercing eyes were sharp as spears: she could well see that after our quarrel I was desperate and forlorn.

'Feeling weary, at the hour of low tide, she appeared disguised as her own servant girl, comforting me with words sweeter than a parrot's. Her walk was as graceful as the swan's, her grace subtler than the peacock's.

'Intoxicated by desire, she danced the brief, lewd dance of lust *(puravai).* Her frail body could not bear ornaments: she danced on the steps of my home to the rhythm of her swaying belt, the music of her ankle bells. She knew I desired her but would not embrace me. She performed the dance of indignation *(kilarvai).* Her innocent forehead was framed by curls of the hair which, with its load of flowers and pearls, whipped her shoulders. The weight of her breasts forced her frail waist to bend. She appeared unconcerned that her tresses were undone. When a messenger placed at her feet a letter telling her my love, she feigned to misunderstand it.

'Then she danced the theme of anguish *(terccivari),* crying out to the four winds the pain caused her by our parting and the unbearable desire that draws her toward me. She committed the impropriety of revealing her anguish to members of my family. Next, wearing a wreath that drew swarms of bees to her, she performed the dance of despair *(katcivari).* She told her misery to all the passers-by. She pretended to faint *(eduttukkolvari),* and, more than once, did lose consciousness. Those into whose arms she fell recalled her to her senses and tried to comfort her.

'But for this girl, adorned with jewels, whom I once dearly loved, such dances are a daily performance. She is only a dancing-girl.'

When Kovalan refused to take the wreath that the beautiful and jewel-laden Madhavi had sent him, and also the message written on its *talai* and pandanus flowers, Vasanta-mala was overwhelmed with grief. She ran to her mistress to tell her all that had happened. But Madhavi of the long flower-eyes answered her:

'Lovely girl, if we do not see him today, he will come tomorrow at dawn.'

Yet with heavy heart she lay sleepless all night on her couch strewn with fresh flowers.

Coda

Vasanta-mala speaks

When Spring comes, the red lotus blooms,
the mango's tender leaves begin to tremble,
the noble ashoka *bursts into flower.*
Who can describe the pain that lingers in
my mistress's tender eyes, shaped like sharp
spears?

The cuckoo trumpeted his command:

'All lovers who have quarrelled
shall rush into each other's arms.
For so does Eros order.'
You enjoyed her tender words
in that enclosure by the sea,
but shut your ears to the appeal she wrote
on those frail petals this day when her heart

was ravished by the frenzy of the Spring.

Canto Nine

The Dream

Evening approached, the day faded away; women, their waists lithe as lianas, scattered grains of paddy and open jasmine buds on the floors of their homes. They lighted lamps studded with glowing gems. And they changed into the clothes they wear at night.

Once, long ago, Malati gave a cup of milk to the young son of the second wife of her lord husband. The boy choked, had spasms in his throat, and died. She was terrified, for she knew that her brahmin husband and his new wife would unquestionably accuse her. She took the dead child in her arms and carried it to the temple where the *kalpaka,* the 'tree of ages,' is worshipped. From there she ran in succession to the temples of the white elephant, the pale god Balarama, the Sun, Shiva the god of the city, Murugan the spear-bearing god of youth, Indra who wields the thunderbolt, and the god who dwells beyond the city walls. She also visited the Jain temple and the temple of the Moon. She beseeched all the gods:

'O mighty ones! Give me your help in my terrible trouble!'

At last Malati reached the sanctuary where the famous god Shattan had made his residence. Shattan was skilled in the art of magic; she resolved to ask his advice. At that moment a young woman appeared—a girl of such startling beauty that she made all others look plain. She said to Malati:

'Innocent girl! The gods do not grant their favours without a sacrifice. This is no lie but the truth. Give me the child.'

With these words, she snatched the dead body from the

startled woman and ran off into the darkness toward the
funeral pyres. There the demon Indakini, ravener of
corpses, seized the child and devoured it. Malati shrieked
like a peacock at the roar of thunder. The divine Shattan
came and tried to console her:

'Mother, be calm! Give up all fear! Look straight before
you and you shall see the child come back to life.'

To fulfil his promise, the god took the form of a boy
asleep beneath the cuckoo-haunted trees. Malati, mad with
joy, grasped this supposititious child. She clasped it to her
heart and brought it back to its mother.

This divine brahmin boy grew up and became learned
in all the sacred scriptures. At his parents' death he
observed with piety the rites to ancestors. He was so wise
that people made him a judge in their quarrels. He married
a woman of uncommon beauty named Devandi. Before
approaching her, he prayed:

'May the flowers of your eyes be able to withstand the
fire of mine!'

One day he revealed to her the fact that he was
immortal, and then, requesting her to visit his temple, he
disappeared. Before he left, he had taught her certain
mysterious magic words. After that, Devandi went each day
to worship him in his sanctuary. To those who asked news
of her husband she would say:

'He has gone on a pilgrimage. If you meet him, please
bring him back to me.'

She had once heard about the unhappy life of virtuous
Kannaki, the loyal wife abandoned by Kovalan; it saddened
her. Bringing to the god an offering of arugu grass and rice,
she beseeched him to intervene. She went to Kannaki,
blessing her:

'May your husband return!'

Kannaki replied:

'He may come back, but my trials will not end. I had a
fearful dream. The two of us were walking hand in hand

toward a vast city. Some people told a lie, so that Kovalan was accused of a crime. When I heard it, I felt as if I had been bitten by a scorpion. I ran to the king, and threatened him and his city with disaster. I should say no more. It may be only a bad dream. O woman with narrow bracelets, when you hear about the harm done to me and its happy results in the end for my husband and me, you may laugh.'

Devandi said:

'Woman with gold anklets! Your husband did not reject you. All this is the result of a vow that remained unfulfilled in a past existence. To counteract the curse that vow has brought upon you, you should visit the sacred site where the Kaveri flows into the sea. Near a few neydals in blossom there are two ponds, dedicated to the sun and moon. Women who bathe in these ponds and then worship the god of love in his temple shall spend all their lives close to their husbands and later enjoy the pleasures of Paradise. So let us go bathe there today.'

Kannaki at once answered the well-meaning woman:

'This plan is not proper: [a married woman should worship no other deity than her husband].'

A few moments later, a young servant approached and said:

'Our dear Kovalan has come to our door. It seems that from now on he will look after us.'

Kovalan entered. He was struck by pain when he saw the pallor of the graceful Kannaki. He said:

'Living near a woman bred on falsehood and for whom truth and untruth are alike, I have lost all the wealth my ancestors gathered. I feel great shame at the dire poverty that I bring into this house today.'

Welcoming him with a clear smile that lit up her face, Kannaki said:

'Do not be anxious: you still possess the gold circlets that weigh on my ankles. Accept this modest gift.'

Kovalan answered:

'Honest girl! I accept these precious ankle bracelets as a new capital from which we shall regain all the jewels and all the riches I have squandered in my folly. Let us get ready, woman with the flower-adorned hair! Come! We shall go to Madurai, a city known for its towering walls.' Inspired by fate, he decided to start at once, before the day should come to disperse the night's dark veil.

Love Poems

Mayura

1

Before your father was a youth I was a young man, yet I
went into the forest when I had seen you, to follow and find
the coupling place of the tigers. His feet about the gilded
one and his rod flushing out to crimson were as nothing to
my youth, who am an old man and a King's poet.

2

A procession of hills no longer impedes me, for I spring over
them, and find the flower-covered bow within my hands. I
discover under my hand the flowery bow of Kama, and
break large branches out of my path. I have seen you, O
daughter of a woman, and I break down branches. I cast
great stones from my way.

'Love Poems' by Mayura from 'Two Sanskrit Lyric Poets: Amaru and
Mayura' in *Eastern Love* Vol. II, edited and translated by E. Powys
Mathers. London, 1927.

3

Doubtless your feet are red with lac; certainly the flowers
grow together to check your feet in the forest. The prints of
the toes of your feet, as I follow, who am now a young man,
are separate and beautiful and red in the dust.

4

Rain-scents of the coupling of the trees come to the
assembly of poets again. You went to bathe in the river, and
I took new interest in the King's stallion. He roared for the
quick mares to be brought to him, he drummed with his
forelegs upon them, O woman moist with a boy's love.

5

A yellow cloud of hornets is about the water-flower, and it
is scented as it lies on the tumult of the pool. Your navel is
a water-flower and lo! there is a cloud of saffron hornets
about it. It is deep to look within, as if the depth of it had
been painted with blue kohl.

6

Venturing I have seen you raise your garment and press
your palms to your ankles, drawing your hands up, as if you
were passing them over tall trees. I have been disturbed by
your straight sweetness from ankle bone to the flower of
your body.

7

Gradually the trees of the new year come down to drink at
the river, and you are there washing between your gold
thighs. You break the water of the pool into moons by
kicking, and then play the fish, going down to kiss the
hidden roots of the water-lilies.

8

No breasts are heavier than these, and yet they are as stable as gourds hardened for wine. Also there are set impregnable crimson castles on the hills of them.

9

I have been hit about the brow by the many sticks of your beauty, your navel had a stick, your haunches a great stick, your hair a bludgeon. I have fainted at the sight of this woman as a boy faints. Your breasts were two clubs, raining upon my head.

10

Let me come out from the poets' assembly and cast about for the traces of your feet in the dust; I am more than any tracker since you came to me with wet arms, since you came to me out of the private chamber. Your feet had the appearance of gold with ten rubies. Your eyes were fainting.

11

Rearing the green flame of his tail, the peacock casts the hen beneath him in the dust of the King's walk. He covers her, and we can hardly see her. She cries and he cries; and the copper moons in the green bonfire of his tail die down; and I am an old man.

12

As you lay on the palace couch of sea-yellow and showed me lovelinesses, saying that they were unimportant, our King was counting his number of gold breastplates and litters woven from bird feathers. I would have made stanzas about your hands.

13

Dust of dead flowers, O tigress, has been spilled smoothly on the body of your breasts. It is a task to praise your breasts, for their tips are gilded like the sun and red like sunset. And I do not know what to think of them.

14

Suavely the wine pouring from your lower lip has called the gold swarm. It is a crimson fruit and has called the bees. The boy who has sucked that carmine fruit is drunken, and I am drunken, and the gilded bees.

15

Early you have plunged as a fire coal into the river pool, the fishes love you, and your breasts displace the water. The demon of the stream, having come down to drink between his tigers, leaps out upon you. He bears you down, and you come up uncooled from the cool river.

16

Now you pout your fruit-red lower lip, O woman with wet hands, to be a comfort to those that thirst. You make me cool with the breathing of your underlip, though crimson lac is afraid before it, and to touch it is annihilation.

17

Old maker of careful stanzas as I am, I am also as the fishmonger's ass and smell to you in riot. He is insensate and does not care though the Royal retinue be passing. He climbs and is not otherwise contented. And he brays aloud.

18

Rapture disturbed the gold water-hornets, they were in a cloud about your navel. It was deep with blue deeps, a flower on the river. It was cut as if with the three strokes of a sharp sword. A child with his hand full of musk unguent could by no means have filled it.

19

Once I told my King that night had fallen, and he said: 'It is as yet noon.' But I insisted, proclaiming: 'Night has descended in long shadows, because that woman has let fall her most heavy hair.' And he said: 'You are an old man, Mayura.'

20

For now I break branches out of my path, seeing that the soles of your feet are red. The rain-scent of the coupling of the trees comes again to the poets' assembly, and your hair is nightfall, and I am an old man.

The Loves of Haralata and Sundarasena

Damodaragupta

There is a great city named Pataliputra; it is the gem which decks the forehead of the world. Sarasvati, Goddess of Wisdom and Learning, dwells there; high over the residences of Indra towers that city. Above it the moon stretches down her rays like white hands, to steal the charms of its women to adorn her lotus; it is as if she felt shame for the stains upon her face and desired to hide them.

In Pataliputra men grow slack to their wives because of the steel-tipped arrows of the moving eyes of the girls with rounded buttocks.

The noble ladies of that place are famed for the delicacy of their discourse, and of their hands and feet; for the purity of their hearts and the instability of their regard; for the firmness of their breasts, for their exceptional regions, and for the great heaviness of their hair; for their natural inclination to their lords and masters, and for the supple graciousness of their waists; for the depth of their sensibility, and of their navels, which are the quivers of love; for the ample expansion of their hinder parts, and for

'The Loves of Haralata and Sundarasena', from 'Lessons of a Bawd' by Damodaragupta in *Eastern Love* Vol. I, edited and translated by E. Powys Mathers. London, 1927.

their ardent veneration of all such men as are worthy of respect.

It was there that Purandara dwelt, who, in his time, was held to be the very home of wisdom. He came of a lofty family and was estimable in all things.

Although he was avid to follow the straight way, although he turned from all human frailty and avoided the wives of others, yet he could not prevent his heart from dreaming a little of women.

Therefore he had a son called Sundarasena, whom the Creator had formed to be a second God of Love. The noble women found it difficult to remain in the paths of virtue when once their glances had fallen upon his beauty. 'Is it the sun himself that such charm should flow thence? Was he made from shining fragments of the moon, that he brings us so much sorrow?' It was with such thoughts that the caravan of local ladies looked upon him, and could come to no decision.

He borrowed a very joyous look from the rays of the moon, and from the mountain its solidity; its haughty movement from the cloud, and depth from the sea.

He was the dwelling of irreproachable conduct, the home of intelligence; the fortress of perseverance, the palace of discourse, and the throne of upright dealing.

He was the adoration of women, the touch-stone of perfection, a benevolent tree upon the arid road of life.

The conversation of upright men delighted him; his criticism of fine tales was in exquisite taste; he was the thicket of desires to all who loved him.

He had a friend as frank and noble as gold, whose name was Gunapalita; they were bound together as ocean and the moon, and shared both pain and pleasure.

As these two were walking in a solitary place, they heard a voice saying these words:

'Those who have not travelled, and are ignorant of the manners, customs, and character of alien peoples, and have thus not learned to pay respect to the respectable, such are as bulls without horns.'

When Sundarasena heard these words, he said to his good friend: 'O Gunapalita, the thoughts of that unknown but upright man are excellent.

'It is only by passing over the earth, girt like a fortress with her moat of seas, that we can learn those things which make up knowledge: the conduct of the brave, the wiles of the wicked, the innumerable characteristics which distinguish men, the pleasant conversation of the cultivated, the wanton discourse of shameless women, the conduct of priests, the practice of sharpers, and the life of harlots.

'Therefore, my friend, put your heart to my heart, for we have exhausted the little pleasure of these places. Let us embark upon a journey together which shall complete our learning and ripen our intelligence.'

But when Sundarasena had spoken so with his whole soul, his friend made answer thus reservedly:

'It gives me as much shame as pain to set an obstacle on the path of another's prayer; but listen, and I will tell you something of a traveller's suffering.

'At the fall of day the voyager drags himself to some village, his body covered with rags, his strength exhausted by the unforeseen length of the day's march, all grey with a layer of dust, and asks for shelter:

'"O mother, O sister, be pitiful, and do not harden your heart against us! Doubtless your sons and brothers are also travelling on business into far lands, and are exiled from the hearth as we are.

'Would we destroy your house before we leave tomorrow? Nay, for when a stranger finds comfortable shelter in the home of excellent persons, he treats that dwelling as his own.

'We would pass the night in any way at all, upon this spot, O mother. See, the sun has already fallen! Whither could we journey further at this hour?"

'Such are the sad words which the poor traveller must repeat from door to door, while the suspicious housewives answer him with arrogance:

'"The master is not at home! You croak for nothing! Go to the temple! . . . It does not matter what one says to these people, they will not depart! The importunate impudence of some folk!"

'And when, after making great difficulty and before the ever increasing vehemence of their prayers, the master of another house has pointed to the corner of a hut, and said disdainfully: "Lie there!" they listen all night to the poor man being tortured by his tender wife: "Why have you given lodging to men we do not know?" and hear him eternally answering: "They seemed unfortunate and quite respectable. What else was I to do?"

'Also a crowd of women will run in from the neighbourhood on the pretence of borrowing a pot or some other thing, but really to find out what is going forward, and to take their sister's part. "You will have to keep an eye on the house," they say. "Many thieves have been seen passing upon the road."

'And, when he has thus visited a hundred houses and has suffered the tortures of privation, the unfortunate traveller will soon come down to begging by the roadside: a meagre handful of rice or beans, of peas or lentils.

'A wanderer's food depends upon the caprice of others: the earth is his bed, the temple is his home, and Destiny has prepared a broken brick to be his pillow.'

He fell silent and waited for Sundarasena to speak; but just at that moment someone chanced to sing these most appropriate verses:

> *To him who journeys with a goal worth proving*
> *What matter the conditions of his roving?*
> *The temple floor shall be a palace to him,*

> *The stony hearth a feather bed to woo him,*
> *And leathery scraps which stay-at-homes abhor*
> *Shall be to him a banquet and much more.*

And when he had heard this singing, the son of Purandara turned with joy to his friend, and cried: 'That unknown man has expressed my heart for me. Come! Let us set forth together!'

It was thus that Sundarasena resolved to go down into a sea of suffering, and take his friend for a companion there. He told his father nothing of his project, but left the flowery city of Pataliputra on that same day.

With his faithful friend he wandered over the whole earth; and in each new country that they found they eagerly collected the discourse of the learned, and exercised themselves in various weapons. They digested the contents of wise books, and were witness of many prodigies. They perfected themselves in painting and sculpture, music and dancing. They became expert in the tortuous ways of knavery, and listened with attention to the gallant speech of courtesans and their lovers.

When they had plumbed to the depth of every science, and had studied each manner of life among many peoples, they turned their feet homewards, and thus came on a certain day to the mount Arbuda.

When Gunapalita saw that his friend wished to pause upon this vantage point of earth, and to look down from it upon the smiling country unfolded beneath his feet, he said to him: 'Let us now look upon this queen of mountains!

'This daughter of the height is rich in running waters. They are cool and clear. Surely they were cast down in pity upon the desert by the glaciers of Himalaya.

'She has the brightness of Shiva; her brow has the grace of the cold rays of the moon. A few solitary penitents live upon her flanks, and the pure air feeds them.

'Hither innocent and fair young girls come in a troop

as if to pluck the stars, astonished to see the stars like buds of fire.

'And by a miracle the seven points of the Great Bear dwell very close to her. Who would not be moved by the sublimity of this enormous rock?

'She leans above the path of the air. Surely she was created that the weary feet of the horses of the sun might find a resting place.

'The grasses, by growing here, have entered into communion with the moon. Might we not follow their example and after due precaution, find out a sweet affinity with God?

'There is no true friendship save in common labour, therefore this mountain pours down the refreshing drops of her cascade about the cosmic elephants, to refresh them at their task of holding our earth in air.

'The men who abide in this loneliness bend all their zealous energies towards the conquest of another life. But though they have stifled inclination in their hearts, they will not wound any creature, even a serpent. Although they feed upon fruits, they are not monkeys; and although they follow their holy pleasure in all things, they find no pleasure in a savage deed. Although they are filled with love and compassion and pity for all who seek refuge among them, yet they rejoice in an utter peace of the spirit.

'Also the land which spreads at the feet of this mountain shines with all pleasant things: it is filled with as ardent light as the path of the Sun god; it is adorned with trees of every kind; it is peopled by monkeys and gazelles and bears and elephants.'

While his companion was thus assisting Sundarasena to admire the beauties of the mountain, and while he himself, in joyful curiosity, banqueted his eyes upon her, he heard some person singing:

Who has not seen Arbuda's flanks
Has but his journey's pain for thanks.

'That man has sung very sensibly,' said Sundarasena. 'Come, my friend, let us climb to the highest of these amiable peaks, that we may enjoy the beauty of their prospect in full.' Soon they reached the summit of Arbuda, and contemplated the dwellings of the wise hermits in delight; their green gardens, their pools and fishponds and small streams. But while they walked thus upon the back of the world, decked out with abundant thickets and with meadows of new flowers, Sundarasena beheld a girl who was strolling and playing games with her companion. She had the swift beauty of the sun, yet the softness of moonlight. She was the Creator's perfect work; she was the crown, the achieved model of all life, the weapon of Kama, a steel to cleave the shield of holiness.

As Sundarasena stood regarding her his heart became disturbed, and he said to himself in admiration and surprise:
'Whence came a Creator of such exquisite cunning that he could unite these contradictory perfections into one girl?

'She is friendly in her aspect, she is a star and without blemish. She has a face of impeccable lotus, and surpasses the lute.

'The shapes and junctions of her body are beyond cavil, and she has high breasts. She borrows her colour from the autumn moon.

'She has haughty attitudes, fine walking, and a mighty region. She takes pride in the noble posture of her feet.'

And even as he felt an invincible inclination towards her, she also fell beneath the hand of Kama.

She leaned forgetful against the root of a tree, and felt the true pain of love flowering upon her body's stem.

The scented magnificence of the garden became accomplice to increase her trouble, for gardens also feel Kama.

Her members, with their veins and joints, were softened, and gave birth to pearls.

She had fallen into the nets of the god, the slight one! Her harmonious body shook in agony! Her fixed regard was lost in emptiness! She was like a silver fish flapping in a wicker snare! She stiffened and trembled and the small hairs of her body stood on end! Her sighs now put her sweat into condition; for the god with the uneven number of darts had so commanded it. With so exceptional a beauty, ah, well, he knew his game.

Her very pain dowered her with sweetest attractions; for her deep sighs moved her breasts enticingly. Her sincere passion added the enchantment of tenderness to her glances; her hidden inclination gave her face new brightness; the charm of trembling words and uncertain walking came from her trouble. But although her beloved was near her side, and although the sharp arrows of Kama rained about her like hail, she dared not speak of the new thing which grasped her heart, for fear of killing it.

Then her friend led her away, for she recognized that lover was looking upon lover, heart burning to heart. Therefore she led her away, saying:

'Alas, alas Haralata! Beware of these movements; a true and candid inclination of the heart augurs no good to a daughter of joy, for the reality of love is forbidden her who lives by her body.

'Despise the man who brings no money, honour the man who has a solid fortune; our beauty is but nature's tool for building riches, O fair innocent.

'If you amuse yourself with love with a handsome boy, and take no regard for profit, then you will be mocked, O beautiful, by all the troops of thoughtful prostitutes.

'Men who stand in glorious youth and are protected by their star, whose good works bear fruit, who carry the desire of joy . . . such men will seek you of themselves, infallibly wounded. Bees are not sought for by the flowering branches.'

But when her friend had thus spoken, Haralata, whose

every limb was torn by the arrows of desire, let indistinct syllables painfully fall from her, in a voice which lacked assurance:

'Dear friend, lend me your cares for the cure of my exceeding trouble, for those who are bound by such are not accessible to reason.

'A lover not yet yoked, a breath of wind, and the soft month of Spring—all these devote our heart to death.'

So Shashiprabha, when she saw the body of her friend thus poisoned by the venom of the snake of love and understood that great misfortune reigned in her heart, went out to find the son of Purandara and, having made him a reverence, spoke to him:

'Although the embarrassment which suits my trade would force a courtesan to silence, yet it is most necessary that this affair be adjusted, and in misfortune, very dear friend, decorum may be discarded.

'Haralata saw you for a moment, and lo! she has fallen already; the god has stricken her.

'He lives within our hearts; his arrows, piercing her shield of stiffened hairs, have found her labouring body.

'What shall the poor child do? Where may she grieve? To whom shall she have recourse, being tortured by the wind which comes from the south?

'The green-billed cuckoos have already broken their vows of silence to make her suffer; they rack her with their jargoning.

'The walk of the tenderly-membered girl now wavers and is uncertain. The swans, unheeding of weariness, rejoice to come and go upon the water.

'Though the honey-fly stifles under the hot sighs of the flower who faints for him, he will not grant her a moment of repose. Love's pain cannot forswear love's happiness.

'*Do not repulse me*—thus the bee makes murmur in his love communion. The flower he woos is at a girl's ear, and pensively, feeling her body weaker, the fair one dreamily hears him: *Do not repulse me.*

'If the gold circlet has fallen from her arm, it is because she has let her hand droop by her side.

'Behold a miracle! The belt of her waist has become undone in her walking, and hangs upon her haunches; but to rest thus on a heavy buttock leads fatally to falling.

'Her collar of evil pearls has entered into intelligence with Kama, although she has often caressed them; they have lighted a sudden fire in the breast of my friend! How can truth come of what is false within!

'The crystal drops of her sweat mingle with the waves of her weeping upon her breasts; they roll through that shadowed valley and feign, because her tears are stained with her eyes' collyrium, the radiant waters of the Ganges mingling with black Yamuna.

'She is surrounded by these: the singing of the green-billed cuckoo, flowers, sweet winds of Spring, love, and the bees; she knows the ascetic martyrdom of five fires.

'Come with me, very dear, and save the child ere the tenth state of love, for that is death. The duty of a noble heart surely, is to those who call upon it.'

Now Gunapalita, as soon as he saw what lively interest his friend accorded to these words, understood that a great love was seeding in his heart, and therefore, because he feared the danger of the sentences he had heard spoken, said to him:

'Although the torrent of love is hard to stem in the cataract of youth, yet these young women pass every man in turn between their hands, and a person of understanding should well consider what end there may be to such relations.

'With public women we meet coquetry at first, then passion and then love, then jealousy, then heartache; they follow the fluctuations of our purses.

'How can a youth of race permit himself attachment with such a woman? She loves the man she has but seen for a moment, and swears he is indeed the first and last!

'A Pradyumna (incarnation of Kama) is ever a Pradyumna to these courtesans, as well you know; an ugly man is ever ugly, a loving boy is ever loving, a fool is ever a fool.

'They hide their regions to augment desire and certainly not through modesty; they wonderfully dress themselves to attract their lovers, not to safeguard the manners of the time.

'They drink meat soup to sustain the efforts of men, and never because they like it. Their skill in painting and each other art serves to set off their wit; it is not their distraction.

'The red of passion is upon their lips, not in their hearts, for those are darker; there is a straightness in their encompassing arms, not in their nature; they are lifted by the pride of heavy breasts, not of their conduct; and it is by conduct that the just discriminate.

'They pay profound attention to their region, round like a mountain, but none to the nobly born whom they have robbed; they are careless in walking, not in their plans to make all men ridiculous; they pay great care to the exclusiveness of their dressing, with its fine colours, but their bodies are common to all men; the drunkenness of love is upon their lips, not tender affection for the meritorious.

'They are full of ardour even for boys; they urge themselves to explosions of passion for old men; even for those who have lost all virile force they have kind looks; even for those of chronic illness they reserve desire.

'Love covers them with drops of sweat, but to his sweetness they are strangers still; they tremble like leaves because of passion, but their hearts are hard as diamond.

'Surely they are like the metre *Jaghanachapala* that gracelessly jigs along; they pass their lives in an irregular agitation of their region; they have not the noble and harmonious grace of the metre *Arya*. They are nourished by others, but the signs of passion in their eyes are feigned; they are learned in giving their limbs to the first comer, but know not how to give their hearts.

'They are unpitying as the ichneumon to the snake, yet smile and smile; although they are lamps of love, in the sweetness of the oil they nothing participate.

'They have this in common with virtue, and this alone: they take exception in their lust to no one; they find their joy through Krishna, yet love Hiranyakashipu, his enemy, gold and delicate dishes, I mean, and the vests of luxury.

'They practise the expediency of princes, they studiously avoid, that is to say, relation with the penniless; they are like man-eating birds.

'They spy upon all men from their doors, and have varied means of action; they seize upon riches; you shall not conquer them.

'Women and bees first coax their victims open, then leech them to the dregs.

'What things have power of attraction and a hard exterior? Women and lodestones.

'Harlots and elephants have this in common: they are ridden by men, and loved for their living devotion; they are well beaten about the hinder parts, and go from one owner to another.

'A public girl may care for the perfect lover, but is like a merchant's scale in this: if you cast the least packet of gold into the balance it swings in your direction.

'Daughters of joy are like rattles with gilded handles, charming without, and hard throughout, and well-nigh hollow.

'Therefore, if a man be so blinded by passion, or lacking in intelligence, or cursed by Destiny, as to join himself with one of these who pass from hand to hand, he is diving with arms held high and head bent forward, into, a pit. . . .'

But while he was lavishing such counsels upon his friend, who stood tormented by the love which grew within

him, a man sang three appropriate couplets in their
neighbourhood:

> *Only a fool's afraid when Kama leads to him*
> *The captive flowery bodies Kama kneads. To him*
> *Alone the single profit of the life of man*
> *Comes not, the gracious quick-thighed strife of man*
> *And woman. Also, know a girl's insistence is*
> *The meed of virtue in our past existences.*

So, when he heard these words, the son of purandara
answered his companion, saying: 'The song of that excellent
man expresses the very feelings of my heart.

'Therefore, O Gunapalita, let us hasten to console this
Haralata; she is torn by the points of the bodiless one; surely
her unquiet eyes are wandering hither and thither. What
useful purpose can be served by hesitation?'

And, while these things were happening, there was a
courtesan down in the house of love who ruthlessly
condemned her lover to the door. She said that he was
jealous, but really she had taken all from him!

Another sulked despairingly because she had worked
for nothing; the garment which her lover had given her
proved of the cheapest.

Another bullied a client who had left without paying
the night before; she had seen him passing in the road; now
red with anger she bitterly reclaimed her due from him.

An old bawd said to a plucked youth daring to show
himself at the door of the house where his rival triumphed:
'Begone, O threadbare dung, O useless body!'

A girl, fulfilled with joy and gold, showed her new
scratches and bites proudly; her struggle had been with a
king's son, and she was uplifted to display such marks of
rare good fortune.

Another girl had seen her night's salary rise up beyond
belief, because of a quarrel between rich and generous

lovers, who each desired to possess her: now she displayed her coins conceitedly; but poor in all else, her friends were rich in ribaldry.

Two lovers had drawn their steel for the eyes of her whom each had chosen for that night; but an ancient procuress zealously came between them.

'Now that I have saved much gold from many lovers, I need some nice young man to share my fortune.' Thus did a bride of all chain down a senile admirer's heart.

A lover, who had lost all for love, now curried favour; he recruited wealthy enthusiasts for those who had maimed him.

'In my running riot for you I have left my hearth, and now you play the stranger!' Thus wailed an unfortunate whose woman would not know him.

A lecher, whose mistress had lain with another, won his case before a tribunal of old rakes; now he was bearing back the double of what he had given her for the night.

'Four days ago I bought her splendid clothes,' complained a lover, 'and now she has nothing but vile words for me. Tell me what I must do, O Madanaka!'

A little further off another said: 'Keli loves me and is tenderly attentive, O Kalahamsaka; but it would take me a hundred years to tame that camel, her mother.'

'Make ready flowers!' a woman was crying. 'Make ready the saffron robe! Of what are you thinking? Today you go to see him dance, Kinjalka.'

A bawd was thus disillusioning a lover: 'She shows you five days' rapture because you have shown her five days' gold; but she is not stifled with love for you, Kandarpaka; you need not be so proud.'

'Sister, this son of a patchwork king now never leaves the house: he prevents the others from coming. The rim of the sacred bath is all taken up by this one naked man; he has no purse and puts an obstacle in the way of trade.'

Sundarasena listened to such discourse of girls and

bawds and customers as he went along; when he came at last to the chamber of his love, he had already learned the organization of a brothel.

Impatiently he entered, and was bathed, as it were, in the tenderness of her welcoming glance.

He lavished almost excessive tokens of respect and honour upon Haralata, until her friend seized an occasion to say to him, with all formality:

'What avails a well-turned and flattering conversation, O delightful boy? Here is love lack! Here Haralata, her life between your hands!

'I pray that your youth may be fortunate together and lively in playing, sweet with affection and abandonment, bold against all obstacles!

I pray that the union of your hearts may last indissoluble, that it may be griefless, full of eternally unslaked desire, careless of shame and free of every veil and fetter, rich in the treasure of a hoarded passion!'

The servants associated themselves with this prayer, and then retired in silence. The flames of confident love ran through the limbs of Sundarasena and Haralata, waiting upon promised lust.

And for these two union began as was most fitting; for it was such as stands at equal height with the power of passion and marches with the inclination of the heart, such as prepares the joy of youth, and is life's fruit. It finds its ornament even in impudicity, its honour in gestures which are not separately beautiful, perfection in an outrage of reserve; it shows respect by carelessness, and proves its well-wishing by seizing the hair; blows are the sign of its affection, and biting a joy; scratches are good fortune, and a crushing of the body, even to murder, consideration's seal; it spreads in greedy kisses, where body presses to body, and gives birth to a soul's desire of utter penetration; it seems to spring from far more than a single love, it is so wildly strong; it seems to burn far more that with a single passion, it seems to flower from more than one desire; the absence of effrontery is a vice and discretion a crime; reflection is an outrage, and reserve a weakness.

That passion took on the proportions of a splendid fire, even as its first spark was blown; who therefore could describe the perfect detail of it when grown so great?

A simple lust is the seal of imbecility. Thus these two decided their erotic problem; therefore they penetrated to the inner mysteries in their gracious study and learned the varieties of love.

When the collision had begun, nought else remained for them; nothing to say or think or hide at all.

Their words of caress in the act were broken and impetuously torn.

They were bound to the whirling wheel. Who could tell over the gestures which the Master taught them? Who could envisage that pyre of authentic passion?

When a vigorous man hastily besieges her graceful body, it is not suffering only that a young girl feels: she conceives joy of it also. Mighty is love!

Whether it be the soul of the lover which hides in the soul of the loved one, or the soul of the loved one which hides in the soul of the lover, we may not know. The feeling of their own existence is not clear to them.

She had shut her eyes and her body remained motionless; she manifested the sign of accomplishment within her, high coronation of the act of love.

Covered with sweat and filled with confusion, she lay there glowing, changed in the radiant disorder of her hair.

And while the two thus abandoned themselves without motion, bathing their bodies in a clam beatitude, night passed and did not weary.

At last Haralatá slowly left the marriage-chamber; she was broken in the fight, and yawned and wavered; her eyes were rosy and hollow and still half-asleep.

Outside the girls were chattering:

'I have been at my little lover's house. We passed the night together in eating, drinking and talking, and, at the very last of the last, we loved each other.'

'A very young and ingenuous brahmin, who is quite stupid and full of sap, and who does not often succeed in obtaining a woman, fell on me like sudden death last night, in the cast off clothes of a lover.'

'Desire does not sleep though strength decays; that wicked old man tormented me with his whims all night; they lead to no end, except when I deceive.'

'When my client fell dead drunk, I leapt into bed; I was able to sleep by myself all night.'

'My lover came to me, thralled by my beauty; he is very smooth in lovemaking, tender in discourse, and rich in pleasant double meanings; O my dear, he is the most seductive creature in the world.'

'An unfortunate fool of a peasant passed the night with me; he stretched his limbs straight in the bed, and turned his face from me; I had made him slack by my prayers, and he hardly dared to sigh; he ran with sweat, and, though he had been satisfied, he could not sleep; he waited for the morning with impatience.'

'Avoid Harisena, O Vilasaka,' another bawd gave counsel. 'Avoid her as far as you can see her coming, blind young man! A magistrate's son, a most dangerous enthusiast, has got his hooks on her.'

'I would kill Kaumaraka in the arms of Matanasena,' a jealous girl was crying, 'but her mother mounts guard too well; I shall never catch them.'

'Why have you left Kuvalayamala's hearth, O Lilotaya?' 'Because there is nothing more for me to do there, brother. No gold, no love!'

'The young man, Manjiraka, whose fortune was stolen from him, now goes to that girl's house for the whole night, and gives her nothing.'

'Balika is still a child,' proclaimed an expert, 'and yet

she eclipses grown women. Her maturity is precocious; it has a proud splendour.'

'Hara, o little hunchback girl,' another was crying, 'tell your pitiless dancing master that the body is a tender thing; ask him why he so labours to strain it out of shape.'

'It is a waste of time to teach that lesson to your parakeet, O Sutaradevi; your lover is outside, listening.'

'Take all this gold, my friend,' said a woman in wonderful dresses to a much too handsome youth; 'Since this tender inclination was born, you have been the master of the life and purse of Kusumadevi.'

'Trust me to get you little Chandralekha,' whispered a procuress. 'Afterwards you may give me whatever trifle you decide.'

'The son of Vasudevabhatta, O my mother, not only gives me nothing, but he is shameless; though I have repulsed him, he uses violence; he takes all the garments of your Suratasena and turns them into gold. He never gave me so much as a cotton rag; the wretched goat eats every robe I have.'

'Listen, my friend: a sort of country bumpkin did the most prodigious things last night; but when I shut my eyes under the spell, he was torn with terror, and cried: "Unhappy that I am! I have killed her!"'

'I bungled my merchandise last night, for I had a king's son who did not know what sort of a place he had strayed into; his soul, moreover, was false and wicked.'

'Would you believe it, dearest, the governor of the city had me haled before him by force as a receiver of stolen goods; everybody saw this; but they found nothing at my house for all their searching.'

'We see you drag your region, Kereli. It is all torn with nail marks. We are sure that you lay last night with a man of the Deccan.

'Indeed, Kereli, the *drop* is upon your lip, the *diamond crown* upon your neck, and the *hare's-leap* upon your breast. Your man was learned in the science of the flowers of love.'

It was to such accompaniment of courtesans' babble, in their freedom from their nightly business, that Sundarasena also went forth from the chamber.

❧

While Sundarasena lived with his mistress in a mirage of youth and passion, fulfilled with that immense attraction which quells the heart, a year and a half passed over him.

One day, as he walked in the park chatting familiarly with his companion, he saw a runner approaching them in rags. This man carried a fan, a gourd, and a leather band upon a stick; his shoes were pierced and his body covered with dust.

The son of Purandara recognized the runner, and murmured meaningly to his friend: 'Dear friend, it is Hanuman.'

The messenger bowed to the earth and placed a letter at Sundarasena's feet. The young man lifted it in haste, and saw that it ran as follows:

'Purandara, from the august city of flowers, addresses his wishes to Sundarasena, but the words are steeped, even to indistinctness, in the dyes of grief and anger.

You have forgotten your stainless race, O one disowned; you have had no thought of what you owed to your elders; you have fallen into the ways of evil, and have not considered the unfavourable reflections which will be passed upon your conduct.

How could a pursuer of girls be born into a race where each has always walked most straightly, and where each has displayed such impeccable conduct that no half-thought could be levelled against it, where each has taken pleasure to do wrong to no man?

You were guaranteed against all evil by the ritual ceremonies of religion, how could you touch the ananthic lips of a harlot?

How should these things accord: a face wet with tears because of the smoke of the three sacred fires, and a sea of weeping at the reproaches of a whore?

How should these things accord: the sacred formula that is murmured during the sacrifice, and the voluptuous whispering, the inarticulate cry of a woman who belongs to all?

How should these things accord: the respectful trembling which seized you when your master beat you with his switch, and resignation under the petulant kicks of an angry girl?

How should these things accord: the antelope vestment of one who gives all his life to pious endeavour, and a garment stained by contact with a public woman?

You split wood for the sacrifices in your childhood; whence came this art to you of tearing mistress' lips?

You practised unwavering obedience to the priest; whence have you learnt this conquering manner over loose women?

Your perfect pronunciation in reciting the syllables of the sacred text became a by-word; whence have you such virtuosity in speech with raging girls?

I have recalled your family to you, now I go pray.'

Sundarasena took note of the contents of this letter, and then fell into a hesitation as to what he should do. Then it was that someone sang these most appropriate lines in the metre *Arya*:

> For him whose eyes are drowned in lust
> Until they miss the way, you must
> Compound a salve of syllables
> The pious mouth of a priest tells.
> Harsh duty and that bitter root

Self-Knowledge should be added to it;
For then the unguent shall sear
And cleanse, and both the eyes see clear.

As soon as Sundarasena's friend, Gunapalita, heard these words, he seized the occasion to say to his companion: 'An upright man is never disparaged because he pays attention to the salutary discourse of dear mouths.

'You have not listened to the counsels of your comrade; your body is plunged into the great deep of evil passions; your surest hope of salvation is in words of an angry father.

'Your Father, the light of his race, who wears his irreproachable conduct as a garment, your father, a man of high-placed heart, is now brought low, Sundara, by the trespass of an evil son.

'Never to have had a son is better than to give the light to evil.

'Virtue cannot hold the hand of happiness. The son by whose transgression a mother is led to cry: *"Would that I had not borne him!"* is an evil son.

'If violent feeling lead us but once from the road, a knowledge of the arts shall stay without fruit, and years passed in the house a master all be barren.

'He at whom people point the finger from afar off, looking upon him and making faces, is dead in life.

'This thing is true, that sensuality cannot be killed. A man of perfect understanding will avoid occasion even of unjust reproach.

'He who cannot waver on that path which the righteous follow, who is the jewel of his family, alone finds happiness. His perfections go out from him into all the world; the upright accord him high consideration; he is sought by the people; he is the throne of good.

'That man who perpetually satisfies his ear with the instructive discourse of his ancestors, the same shall become a treasury of education, knowing the suitable from the unsuitable.

'When a youth attaches himself to vile women, it is the ripening of the fruit of evil works in a past existence. A noble wife is an abiding joy.

'When he is vexed, she is vexed also; when he is joyful, she rejoices; when he is uneasy, she betrays uneasiness; she is his mirror. But when he is angry, she is afraid, and is careful not to become angry also.

'She allows him as much as he wishes of the amorous gymnastic; she does not forbid his pleasures upon her; she is adroit to slip into his thoughts; she is the inheritance of a treasure of merits in a former existence.'

❧

It was after this that Sundarasena resolved to make his father's house at one again by breaking with his mistress; therefore he said to her, by way of beginning:

'O child of beautiful teeth, you must think no more upon any wounding words which I may have spoken, either in amorous anger or ill-considered pleasantry, or through misunderstanding.

'My heart is laid in yours, as it were a pledge; and to keep a pledge is a very serious matter. Bend all your cares that my pledge shall not lessen in value because of the place of its deposit.'

When her lover had finished speaking, Haralata answered with difficulty, in a hesitant voice, mingling a wave of tears into her words:

'How should these things accord: a woman born of an impure race, who gains her food by giving up her body, whose conduct is deceit, who sells her beauty, and you whose life is one perfection?

'Desire urged you to see the land of lust, and you have stayed here many days. This was because I acquired merit in some other life . . .

'All those sweet pleasantries, those fine double

meanings, those hours consumed in loving conversation . . . you must not keep silence about them in your heart if you would live at peace . . .

'I beg you to pardon me all the harm I have done you, either by negligence or through excess of love, and also all annoyance.

'The roads are hard to go over; you will sleep far from here tonight; no heart is steady. Gunapalita, as he travels beside you, must not be light-hearted.

'When two young folk, whose hearts have at any time been one, know separation, that is the opportunity of a third party to carry them comfort.

'The man who is bound by a tender inclination, a discreet rapture, can abide parting through death or the judgement of the wise alone.'

Sundarasena had listened to her conversation with manifest coldness, and now he said: 'I must depart, my dear.'

With that he turned his head and went away.

But Haralata stayed where she was, leaning against the branch of a banyan, her lips withering under a hot sigh. With fixed eyes she watched her lover go, and then fell heavily to the earth, like a dead stem, straining the fingers of her hand over her broken heart. O end of gracious jesting! She was stricken to death in the innermost of her body, her soul was as empty as sand. 'O spirits of my life,' she murmured, 'do not depart straight away! Remain until he has passed into the trees!' But as she spoke, life left her.

A little later the son of Purandara questioned a traveller who overtook him on the way, saying: 'Have you encountered a grief-stricken woman?'

'Under a banyan tree,' answered the man, 'there lies one, but her beautiful limbs are quiet in death. I have not seen another.'

Wounded in the full of the heart by the shock of these words, Sundarasena fell, and to his friend who lifted him, he showed the ulceration of his heart:

'Be satisfied, O father, and, you, very dear friend . . . . Let joy be manifest! Two things abandoned Haralata at the same moment, this wretch who is I, and her dear life.

'Love delight, the model of constancy, is beaten down. Love's gentle game is over. You spread a light upon me; where is it now?

'O folly of love, depart into the woods, a penitent! The dumb signs have left her. You had sweet shame before your lover's tenderness, you had a noble indifference under his caresses. You concealed so tender, so sweetly foolish a passion. Alas, have you fainted for ever?

'I will return, I will see her again who has perished of our separation; I owe her the last office, I will give her body to the fire.'

He went back to the place where she was dead, and rolled upon the earth; and while his friend strove to bear him up, he cried:

'See, we have come back. Now let your anger fall. Spare me one word, O sulky one. Rise up, my dear! Why do you stay in bed so long, for the bed is dust?

'Why do you not answer me, why do your eyes stay shut? We are lost, and it was through my fault, because you did not wish me to go.

'Now you have climbed into the sky, now you eclipse all women in the city of the king, now Kama is disarmed for all his arrows.

'All over the world it is said: *False as a harlot*. But, with your death, my beloved, the proverb dies.

'Only the son of Shiva, Mahasena, is worthy of our praise at all, for he is eternally chaste, his heart is intangible by love and the eyes of women.

'O porter of the world, why have you opened the gates to my mistress? Did you not know that she was the ornament of the Earth, and that her departing has left it empty?

'Do not burn the Earth's high jewel, O god of fire; it cost the Creator too much pain. Do not steal away the quintessence of the sweet sea!'

Without paying further attention to the lamentations of his friend, Gunapalita now raised a pyre and burnt the body of the courtesan.

In his despair the lover would have thrown himself among the flames, but at that moment a man felt these most appropriate lines rising within his soul, and so gave voice to them:

> *Only a madman follows into death*
> *The girl who seemed more dear to him than breath,*
> *Whose passing puts his soul into confusion;*
> *Since, though in women such an end is meet,*
> *Man has the fortitude to clear his feet*
> *Of every grief, for grieving is illusion.*

These words drew Sundarasena from his prostration, and he said to his friend: 'My spirit is enlightened by this wise man, for he has shown me what is fitting.

'What man of sense would fall into any passion because of this circle of existences? He is bound within it to the pain of losing; he is bound to birth, to age, to sickness and to death!

'Let us go now towards Kusumapura, for I vow to find my refuge in the last stage of life which is asceticism, so that freedom from ignorance may be my portion.'

To this his noble young friend made answer:

'Since earliest childhood you have not left me. What need is there, even for one who dreams of complete renunciation, to abandon a friend? I have not one desire which points towards the world of sense.'

'It is well!' cried Sundarasena, and led his friend in the direction of the forest of penitents, of resolution and abiding vows. . . .

The Queen and the Mahout

Janna

Canto Two

'Listen, this is our story'

The Land of Avanti
shone
like the fair face of a woman,
its main city, Ujjayini,
like her nose—delicate as a bud.
Its King Yasaugha, a great
conqueror, had won renown
for personal valour, and trophies
in war. The princes of the earth
bowed at his feet, and the gems
in their crowns, as they bowed,
burned like lamps
of amethyst around the feet.

'The Queen and the Mahout', from *Tale of the Glory-Bearers: The Episode of Candasasana* by Janna, translated by T.R.S. Sharma. New Delhi: Penguin Books, 1994. The original Penguin edition carried diacritical marks. These have been dispensed with in this edition for the purpose of standardization.

Candramati was the royal queen,
the king's lovely woman.
The king's eyes stood waiting
on her like bodyguards, his mind
adorned her as a jewel. The very
goddess Wealth, the royal deity,
was her maid. She was every
inch a queen. They loved each
other, shared the joys of their bed.
The moon kept watch at their door
by night; the spring, brought on
by the roll of seasons, by day.
And the love-god Mara all day long.

Presently, to the king and queen
was born a son, Yasodhara.
He was comely, radiant as
the arrow of Mara who
brings it out with grace
to fit his sugarcane-bow
and the string made of flowerbuds.
The child, ruddy of limb,
of bright looks, romped about
and brought riches to the eyes that looked,
honey to the lips
that touched him
and himself
to the arms that stretched
                        for a caress.

Years passed. The boy grew
into a fine strapping man.
Were there eyes around, then, one
wondered, that wouldn't tell
how he himself looked like Mara
or like a piece of moonlight

to intrigue us
or touched us with the cool
of a mountain breeze?
Soon he excelled in valour
over enemies who began to feel
the pressure of his sinewy arms.
Presently Mara came along,
this time as hunter
with a decoy to lure
the young prince. The charming
decoy was none other than Amritamati,
now the beloved of Yasodhara.
   And they came together as man and wife.

King Yasaugha, as he grew older,
and greedier for conjugal pleasure,
crowned king his son Yasodhara
and freed himself from the affairs
of State—so that he could bury
himself deeper in voluptuous life.
By and by his hair turned
silver, crept out like a dove
to catch the thieving old-timer
as if with a lamp in hand—
which was an ill-omen, as the
royal custom ran, that
when a dove enters the palace
the king should leave it. Age had
seized Yasaugha, the silver hair
was hint enough for him
to put aside his palace pleasures
and take to the life of a recluse for
the rest of his days. He left his kingdom
to the care of his beloved son, and with
the pick of his men, all of the royal house,
he betook himself to the forest with

the liberty of an elephant
     that breaks loose from its chains.

The realm, divorced from her
rightful master, flew into
the clasp of Yasodhara as a mistress
would when times change.
She now found in his eminence
the cool of sandal and
in his loving care her lost comforts.
The lands he conquered, the trophies
he won, all his victories
he bore about him with ease.
For victory is a clever wench
who breaks her troth with kings
and flies to any new-glossed prince
who comes to the fore by strength of sword.

Young Yasodhara was happy in
the company of Queen Amritamati,
whose looks were the very glass wherein
he dressed himself, and touched his features.
But things soon began to take
a new turn in the young prince's life.

Once, as it happened,
the king discharged his court duties
before time, and by the end
of day, went up the staircase
to the bed-chamber
to meet his beloved queen.
From the casements
rose a tiny column of
incense smoke like the grey-
winged dove that flew out, as if
at the behest of the love-god Mara,

to carry his message to
the minds of people.

Bees came hovering
round for the scent, and
the brush of their wings raised
the musk and camphor dust.
The blue sapphires
adorning the chamber
burned and glowed.
The bed breathed passion. It was
a swing-bed and at either
end were images of swans
inlaid with nine varieties of gems.

There they lay,
the young king and the lovely queen,
in bed in each other's arms.
their eyes, cast, bit
into each other, their bodies
melted in the clasp, like those
fabled moon-stones
when the moon's rays fell on them.
As dolls with strings, the love-god
Mara pulled them, put them
together, and let them get
drunk with the joys of love.
They played as if possessed
by an untiring love for
each other. Tired out at last
in the night's toil, they drowsed
and lay asleep—their bodies
still clinging together loosely, and
drops of sweat running down them.
Yet they didn't have the heart to unclasp!

('listen now, my king,
what happened next')

In the small hours
of the morning, when the noise
of the last change of guards
at the palace gate died out,
the queen heard
a faint voice, and
was awakened. Enclosed
and lost
in the prison of her love's arms,
she heard:
the voice grew into a song,
sweet and alluring in the dark silence.
It came to her
                like fallen seeds
trouble the resting waters.
A tiny ripple
stirred
and grew. Soon it touched
her, tapped her gently, and
woke her out of her drowsy
slumbers. Eyes wide open,
she stared in the dark,
and toward the direction of the song.
The voice came from the nearby
elephant stables. The song
went home to her, shook
her to the roots. Tired though
she was, her body rose again
tingling and all alive to the song.
She lost her heart to it,
to the possessor of that
divine voice. She paid him
                in her mind

the tribute
>of her entire body.

The mahout down in the elephant
stables was a born singer. His voice,
tremulous
and sensitive to the
minutest crease of fancy
dithered,
>wavered,
and answered
to the metamorphic
variations of the tune.
Keeping time,
>working
to a climax,
the song took a stance
>stood poised
limned,
and limbered away to the end.
The voice came
>smooth and vivid
to the queen as if
she had touched it.
Lured
and lost in the song
there now broke out within her
a cascade of feeling,
an irresistible urge to see him,
touch him, be one with him.
The anguish continued till daybreak.

In the morning
the queen held the hand
of her pet maid, and led her
to the private chamber

to tell her of her heart's deep desire.
She begged of her
to fly forthwith to the mahout,
and fly back to her with the news
of an arranged tryst with him.

The maid left for the mahout
and found him drowsing
in the elephant stables. She stood
for a moment, hesitant, and
looked again
at the slouching figure
                    inside the stables.
His face turned her stomach, and
sent her fleeing to her mistress.
The maid wondered
what eyeless Destiny
had sealed this troth.
For shame,
the love of a most lovely queen
to be put into the hands
of the most abhorred slave!
How true the popular saying is,
she felt, that woman wastes her precious love
often on the most unworthy!

The queen was all ears, waiting
to catch the slightest footfall.
Her lips trembled and were charred
from anguish. The maid came back
and saw her all keyed up, her
eager face burning to hear the love's
message. The maid ran her eyes
over her tall lithe figure
that shone
like the splendour of the love-god's rapier.

She came up to the queen and began:
       'O my mistress,
       where on earth did you find this,
       your charmer, I wonder. Surely,
       there can't be a man in all the worlds
       who can be a match to him.'
But the irony was lost on her.
       'My dear, tell me straight,
       don't tease me, is he fair
       and good-looking?
       Don't kill me with silly chatter.'
       'Mistress,' the maid began,
       'If you insist, here it is.
       His features are—O let me count
       and list them on their merits:
       a bald pate, dented forehead, and
       sore eyes, a mouth that has gathered
       the scum of ages round its corners.
       His nose is bashed in, his ears
       are crumpled, and wide spaces run
       between his teeth. His neck has shrunk
       into his chest, the chest in turn
       has fallen and is distressingly narrow.
       He smells like carrion dug out,
       running sore and putrid. And—
       to add to the virtues—
       a hunch-back sits crowning his figure.
       The mahout is, in truth, a perfect
       gnarled stump.'

Amritamati looked, for a moment,
bewildered like a hind
caught in the range of the hunter's arrow.
She felt choked in her throat,
tears welled up in her eyes,
and her heart beat faster.

Nevertheless, passion raged
within her. She said:

  'Dear maid,
  who would cast aside musk
  because it is black,
  sandal
  because its wood is gnarled,
  and scorn the rainbow though
  its back is bent?
  You silly, old-fashioned girl,
  the very vices in the person
  we love turn into virtues.
  Yes, it's true, we ask for good looks,
  nice figure in men if we wish
  to fall in love with them. But once
  in love, and lost in your man,
  why make a fetish of good looks!
  The thing accomplished,
  who would worry about its cause?
  Today he's my god, my all, I see
  in him the very moon and stars
      and the love-god resident.'

The queen put her hands round her,
tipped her well, begged her to
arrange a tryst with the mahout.
The maid, clever as she was, fixed
and managed the affair deftly.
She brought them together at
the appointed time in the elephant
stables. The queen had her heart's
desire fulfilled. She had her fill
of the mahout, day after day.
Like the crow
that tastes and relishes the neem sprouts
and scorns to go near the mango,
Queen Amritamati found her love

for the royal husband fast waning.

A routine love continued, however,
between the king and queen. The king
felt keenly, whenever their eyes met
or they spoke or with mouth to mouth
they sat, there was something missing.
There was no longer the fire, the love
that burned together on their lips.
He would make sure of the cause, he thought,
and know why the queen was listless,
and far off even when
he held her close in his arms.

One night
the king went early to bed,
pretended he was fast asleep.
Amritamati lay beside him, enclosed
in his arms, waiting for the hour of tryst.
The night was well past,
she looked at Yasodhara, his sleeping face.
She stirred a little, and
gently slipped out from beneath
the encircling arms. Like the bee
that slips out from the cup of
a waterlily unfurling into flower
with the advent of night. She took
her steps stealthily from bed,
tiptoed across the chamber down
to the stables. Like Nemesis
that comes in the wake of every vice,
the king too rose up, kept pace behind her,
his hand clasping the hilt of his sword.
As he followed her, he drew out his sword
from the sheath, but kept on behind her.

Tonight Amritamati had come late, and
her paramour was furious.
He wasn't the one to take such a delay
with composure. The queen found
her way in the dark, and went up
to the mahout. Her hand carried
a silver plate with flower-wreaths,
sandal paste and the betel leaves,
all neatly arranged on it.
The mahout shot out his hand in a rage
and caught her by the forelock;
like the hawk that swoops down on a swan,
he knocked her down. The silver plate
came crashing down, the contents lay
scattered on the stone floor. He tugged
fiercely at her hair, and with
a ropewhip lashed her till she fell faint.
He kicked her when she went down
rolling in the dust and
like a watersnake,
writhed at his feet.
A moment later,
Amritamati raised her face,
and begging with her eyes, began:

> 'My love, my master, it's true
> I'm late, but not without reason.
> My husband, the fiend he is, sat me
> on his lap and plied his caresses on me.
> I sat biding time, couldn't help it.
> You're my all, Oh, how I hunger
> for the sound of your voice,
> your shape which always fills my eyes.
> Listen, if you desert me now,
>> this would be my end . . .
> I look upon all men but you as brothers.'

This was too much for the king
who stood in the dark
silently watching the scene. It was
beyond all bounds of human restraint.
The steel whipped up in his hand,
and would have chopped them to pieces.
His arm tingled with the weight
of the purpose that lay before him.
He made as if to strike. But something
held him back; courage, discernment
gripped him from within, and kept him
counsel, saved him from committing
the rash deed. Soon a deep unrest
set in, and he felt disgust
                           at the whole event.

He thought to himself:
Should this hand of mine that bears the sword
to destroy enemy kings kill
these insects that wriggle in the mire?
Would not an elephant look out
for his equal and pass by a tiny ant?
Would a lion attack a fox
and let go an elephant?
It's unjust to kill
the nerveless and the weak-kneed.
This sword that bears the brunt
of battles, and is baptized
in blood, should not be made now
to bear the blood-taint
of these vermin. The renown
that extends to the world's
four corners should not in the end
go down smudged by a worthless deed.
. . . It's true woman goes astray,
shakes off her former love and

flies to the arms of another. But I
cannot undo the stolen love
by killing her. O, this is heinous!
I must spare her. It's only proper
I give her up entirely for lost.
It's conquest to leave her
unconquered, to leave her alone.
I'll not kill him or her, the faithless
woman, and end up with her in Hell.
The king pulled himself together,
turned back and made his way quietly
to his bed. As he lay, Amritamati
returned from her lover on tiptoe, and
thought the king was fast asleep. She got in
silently and lay beside him.

Moments later the king turned a little
to her side, and felt her breasts touch him.
They were once smooth and yielding, he felt,
but now they seemed hard and repulsive.
A mere touch of hers was, once, enough
to send him into rapture. But today
it sickened him. His love was lost
like the milk that turns whey-sour
    by a tamarind drop.

     ⁊

When the boy Abhayaruci came
to this part of the story, King Maridatta
who had till now listened in silence,
couldn't help break out in a rage:
   'Oh, it's all Destiny's doing,
   turning the queen away from a man
   who was in every limb and feature
   the very love-god, Mara,

and driving her to the arms of
a crooked slave! Oh, if only
I could meet that Destiny in some form,
I'll chop up his nose and
rub off the rest by a brick's end.'
To this the boy rejoined:
    'My lord the king,
    no man is a match
    to Mara when the latter comes upon him
    charged with the caprice of Destiny.
    And when Mara with his lure gets
    the favour of slender
    frail-souled women,
    would he let go the chance of galloping
    o'er the noses of dignified men,
    to trip them up from behind, and
    mock their power, beauty, and grace?
    The lure of Mara and the glamour
    of woman, both, in short,
    caused the downfall of Yasodhara.'

So saying, the boy continued the story.

Young Yasodhara broke out in anguish:
One's loved wife is tainted.
Oh, offer it all at the altar
of Mari—this vain talk of loving
and being loved by woman!
Burn all these riches,
make a bonfire of them!
Can the woman I love,
loving another, bring peace to me?
Better is it to love that
which is lasting, the joyous
Liberation, to court Her

who liberates. No more
this loving of wives, truce with them!
Such were the thoughts that passed
and repassed in his mind, as
he kept awake all night,
and lay beside the queen—till daybreak.

When the ceremonial pipe and drum
sounded the morning benediction
in the royal precincts, the king
awoke and left the bed.
He went through the day's routine,
performed the kingly rites and
gave the day's charity.
He went to the ghee-pot
(as part of the custom),
and looked in to catch his reflection
in the warm liquid.
He went to the byre,
ran his loving hand over the pet
rust-coloured cow and its calf.
He held a brief customary levee
with his close officials and
                made for the queen's apartments.

He entered the queen's private chamber
in a lover's humour. He talked to her,
laughed with a light heart.
In frolic
he reached out for her ear,
for the waterlily that adorned it,
and struck her with the flower-stalk.
Feigning the stroke was too hard
for her delicate flesh to bear
she fell down in a faint—
like the fainting bee

caught in the champak's perfume!
Looking intently
at the fine make-believe
the queen enacted,
the king bent over her, saying!
'O dear,
haven't I hurt you,
so frail-limbed!
Give her a hand and
lift her up tenderly!'
He put out his arm
to help to her feet.
But the decrees of fate are strange!
It was fate that now turned death
away from her door to wait at his;
the lily stalk that adorned her ear
turned into a weapon to kill the king!
The queen thought
that her lord must be in the know of things:
Her previous night's affair
with the mahout who beat her,
her stolen amours,
her mean and wretched ways,
all must have seen the light of day!
She still lay on the ground
scared, as if in a swoon.
The king eyed her lying still,
still feigning and keeping up the role.
Suddenly, filled with disgust,
he left her and betook himself
to the far end of the palace,
to his mother's chamber.

*(The queen loses no time in poisoning the king and his
mother, feeding them with dishes of spiced rice mixed with
poison.—ed.)*

Kathamukha

Somadeva

This immortal story came from the mouth of Shiva, arising from his love for Parvati, just as the nectar of immortality arose when the ocean was churned by Mt. Mandara. Those who drink from the immortality of this story shall have their obstacles removed and shall be prosperous and Shiva's grace will bestow godliness on them, even as they live here on earth.

May Shiva's sweat protect you, that water which is fresh from his embrace with Parvati and that is Kama's weapon against Shiva's fiery third eye!

In the kingdom of Vatsa, King Shatanika ruled wisely and well from his capital city Kaushambi. He was descended from the heroic Pandavas, for he was the son of Janamejaya. Although he had two virtuous wives, the Earth herself and the queen Vishnumati, the king had no sons. One day while he was out hunting, he met the sage Shandilya who gave him an oblation for his wife to consume and the prince Sahasranika was born. King Shatanika,

'Kathamukha', from *Tales from the Kathasaritsagara* by Somadeva, translated by Arshia Sattar. New Delhi: Penguin Books, 1994. The original Penguin edition carried diacritical marks. These have been dispensed with in this edition for the purpose of standardization.

well-known for his valour, was called by Indra to help subdue the asuras. *He was killed in battle and Sahasranika became king. Because of his affection for Shatanika, Indra invited Sahasranika to the great celebration that followed the victory over the* asuras. *When Sahasranika saw the beautiful celestial women in Nandana, Indra's paradise, he realized that he should get married. Indra told him that there was already a wife ordained for him since Sahasranika was none other than a cursed* vasu. *His celestial love had also been born on earth as the princess Mrigavati. But when Sahasranika was leaving Nandana, he inadvertently snubbed the beautiful* apsara *Tilottama by ignoring her and she cursed him to be separated from his beloved for fourteen years.*

Sahasranika married Mrigavati, and in time she became pregnant. During her pregnancy, she had the urge to bathe in a tank of blood and while she was bathing, Garuda saw her and thought she was a piece of meat and carried her away. He left her on a mountain where she was rescued by an ascetic and her son Udayana was born in a hermitage. When the child was born, a disembodied voice announced that his son would be king of the vidyadharas. *Udayana grew up strong and brave and learned in all the sciences and his mother gave him his father's bracelet to wear. One day Udayana gave the bracelet to a hunter who had saved his life. The hunter sold the bracelet in the city and it was brought to the king's attention. The time for Sahasranika's curse of separation was at an end and he went to the mountain hermitage to meet his wife and son. With great joy, he brought them back to Kaushambi.*

Udayana was anointed crown prince and Yaugandharayana, Rumanvat and Vasantaka were appointed his ministers. King Sahasranika soon retired to the forest and Udayana ruled his kingdom wisely and well for some time. Gradually, he left all the administrative responsibilities to his ministers and began to spend more and more time in the pursuit of royal pleasures like wine, music and hunting. But soon he began to hear about the virtues and beauty of the princess Vasavadatta and felt that she would be a suitable wife for him. Vasavadatta's father, King Candamahasena, was also interested in Udayana as a son-in-law and decided to take him prisoner so that he would marry Vasavadatta. Udayana was taken prisoner while he was hunting and the king made him Vasavadatta's music teacher. Meanwhile, Yaugandharayana and Rumanvat devised a plan to kidnap Udayana and Vasavadatta so that they could be married, for they were already in love with each other.

When Udayana and Vasavadatta had run away as a part of his ministers' plan, they were often despondent. On one such occasion, Vasantaka told a story for princess Vasavadatta's amusement, a story that was funny and included a great many things.

The Courtesan Who Fell in Love

'There is a city named Mathura, which is the birthplace of Krishna, and a famous courtesan, Rupinika, lived there. Her mother, Makaradanshtra, was an old madame and she appeared like a lump of poison to the young men who were attracted to her charming daughter. One day when Rupinika went to the temple at the time of worship to perform her duties, she saw a young man from a distance. That handsome young man affected her so deeply that she forgot all that her mother had taught her. She told her maid to urge the young man to visit her house that very day and the maid did as she was instructed. The man considered the invitation and then he said, "I am a Brahmin named Lohajangha and I have no money at all. What would I do in the house of Rupinika which is a place that only the rich can enter?" "My mistress does not want your money," replied the maid and Lohajangha agreed to visit the house later.

'Rupinika was thrilled when she heard from her maid that Lohajangha would come and see her. She went home and kept watch over the road that he would take and soon, Lohajangha arrived. When Makaradanshtra saw him she wondered where he had come from. Rupinika rose and went to welcome Lohajangha herself with great respect. She put her arms around his neck and led him into her private apartments. She was completely overwhelmed by Lohajangha's many virtues and felt that she had been born only to love him. She gave up the company of other men and Lohajangha lived happily in her house.

'Makaradanshtra, who had trained many courtesans, was very irritated with these developments and spoke to Rupinika privately. "Daughter, why do you keep the company of this poor man? A good courtesan would rather touch a corpse than a pauper! What can love possibly mean to a courtesan? Why have you forgotten this basic principle of your trade? The beauty of a sunset lasts only as long as the twilight and so also the beauty of a courtesan is short-lived. A courtesan should be like an actress and feign love so that she can acquire wealth. Get rid of this poor man before you destroy yourself!" Rupinika replied in anger, "Stop talking like this! I love this man more than I do my own life! I have enough wealth already, what will I do with more? Mother, you must never speak to me about this again!" Makaradanshtra was very angry when she heard her daughter's words and began to think of a way to get rid of Lohajangha.

'One day Makaradanshtra saw a nobleman coming down the road. He had lost all his wealth but was surrounded by his retainers who were carrying swords. She rushed up to him, took him aside and said, "My house has been occupied by a penniless lover. Come there today and behave such that he leaves at once. Then you can enjoy my daughter tonight!" The nobleman agreed and went into her house. Rupinika was at the temple at that time and Lohajangha had gone out somewhere. Suspecting nothing, Lohajangha came home a short while later and at once the nobleman's servants fell upon him, kicking and beating him all over his body. They threw him into a filthy ditch and Lohajangha escaped from there with great difficulty. Rupinika was overcome by sorrow when she learned of what had happened. The nobleman saw this and left the way he had come.

'Lohajangha, who had suffered the old woman's intolerable atrocities, went to a pilgrimage spot, ready to give up his life for he could not bear to live without his beloved. He wandered in the desert, his heart burning with anger against Makaradanshtra and his skin burning with the heat of the sun. He looked around for some shade but he could not see a single tree. He came upon the carcass of an elephant that had been stripped of all its flesh by jackals. The body was like a shell with only the skin remaining and Lohajangha crawled into it and fell asleep. The breeze blew through the carcass and kept it cool. Suddenly, fierce clouds gathered and the rain began to pour down. The elephant's hide shrank and there was no longer a way out of it. Soon the area flooded and the hide was swept away by the force of the water. It was carried into the Ganga and from there it floated into the ocean. A bird descended from the family of Garuda saw the hide and picked it up, carrying it to the other side of the ocean. It ripped it open to eat it but when it saw a man inside, it dropped it right there and flew away.

Lohajangha In Lanka

'Lohajangha was roused from his sleep by the bird pecking at the hide and he crawled out of the hole made by the bird's beak. He was astonished to find himself on the far shore of the ocean and was quite sure that he had dreamt everything. Then he saw two terrifying *rakshasas* who were eyeing him from a distance with fear. They remembered how they had been defeated by Rama and when they saw that Lohajangha was another mortal who had crossed the sea, their hearts were filled with fear. They discussed the matter amongst themselves and then one of them went and reported the incident to King Vibhishana. Vibhishana, who had also seen Rama's power, was equally frightened at the arrival of another human and said to the *rakshasa*, "Go, my friend, and speak affectionately to that man. Tell him to honour me by coming to my palace."

'The *rakshasa* cautiously went up to Lohajangha and told him of Vibhishana's invitation. Lohajangha accepted calmly and went with the *rakshasa* to Lanka and when he reached there, he was astonished at the number of golden buildings. He entered the royal palace and saw Vibhishana who welcomed him. The Brahmin Lohajangha blessed the king and Vibhishana asked him how he had got to Lanka. Lohajangha cleverly replied, "I am a Brahmin named Lohajangha and I come from Mathura. I was very poor and so I went to Vishnu's temple and propitiated him with severe penances and fasts. Vishnu came to me in a dream and said, 'Go to Vibhishana. He is my faithful devotee and he will give you much wealth.' I said that Vibhishana lived in a place that I could not reach and then Vishnu said, 'You shall see Vibhishana today!' When I awoke, I found myself on the other side of the ocean. I have no idea how I got here."

'Vibhishana knew that Lanka was inaccessible so when he heard Lohajangha's story, he thought to himself, "This man has divine powers!" and he said aloud to the Brahmin, "Stay here and I will give you lots of wealth!" He placed Lohajangha in the care of some man-eating *rakshasas* and he sent others to the Svarnamula mountain to fetch a young bird born in the family of Garuda. He gave the bird to Lohajangha so that he could get used to riding it in anticipation of his long journey back to Mathura. Lohajangha rode the bird around and rested in Lanka for some time, enjoying Vibhishana's hospitality.

Why The Ground In Lanka Is Made Of Wood

'One day he asked Vibhishana why the ground in Lanka was made of wood. Vibhishana explained, "Listen and I will tell you about this since you are curious. Long ago, Garuda, the son of Kashyapa, was eager to free his mother from slavery to the snakes that she had to endure to fulfil a promise. He wanted to eat something that would increase his strength as he prepared to fetch the elixir which would release his mother. Garuda went to his father who said to him, 'Son, there is a huge elephant and a huge tortoise at the bottom of the ocean. They are in this form because they have been cursed. Go and eat them.' Garuda brought them out to eat and perched on a branch of the *kalpavriksha*. The branch collapsed under his weight but Garuda held it in his beak out of respect for the *Valakhilyas* who were practising austerities there. Afraid that if he dropped the branch human beings would be crushed, Garuda took the advice of his father and put it down in an uninhabited place. Lanka was built on that branch and the ground here is therefore wooden." Lohajangha was very pleased with Vibhishana's story.

Lohajangha Outwits Makaradanshtra

'Lohajangha wanted to return to Mathura and Vibhishana gave him many valuable jewels. Since Vibhishana was also a devotee of Vishnu who lived in Mathura, he gave Lohajangha a lotus, mace, discus and conch shell all made of gold to offer to the god. Lohajangha took all that Vibhishana had given him and climbed onto the bird that could travel one hundred thousand *yojanas*. He rose into the sky from Lanka and crossed the ocean, arriving in Mathura with no trouble at all. He came down from the air near a deserted monastery outside the city and hid all his jewels there. He tied up the bird and went to the marketplace where he sold one of the jewels. He bought clothes and food with the money and returned to the monastery. He then ate, fed the bird and adorned himself with new clothes, flowers and sweet perfumes.

'When night came, he picked up the lotus, mace, discus and conch shell, mounted the bird and flew to Rupinika's house. He hovered in the air over the place that he knew so well and made a low sound to attract his beloved, who was alone. Rupinika came out as soon as she heard the sound and saw, hovering in the night sky, a being shining with jewels who appeared to be Vishnu. "I am Vishnu and I have come here for your sake!" he said and Rupinika bowed her head and asked for his blessings. Lohajangha came down from the sky and tied up his bird. Then he went with Rupinika into her private apartments. He stayed with her for some time and then he came out, climbed onto the bird and flew away through the air.

'The next morning Rupinika maintained a strict silence, thinking, "I am the wife of Vishnu. I can no longer speak to mere mortals!" Her mother asked her why she was behaving in this peculiar fashion and after much questioning, Rupinika placed a curtain between herself and her mother and recounted what had happened the night before and the reason for her silence. Makaradanshtra did not believe a word of what her daughter said until that night when she saw Lohajangha arriving on his bird. Early the next morning she went to her daughter, who was still behind the curtain, and said quietly, "Daughter, you have attained the status of a goddess here on earth because Vishnu has chosen you. I am your mother in this world! Grant me a favour for having given birth to you. Ask Vishnu to take me to heaven now, even in this tired old body."

'Rupinika agreed and when Lohajangha came to her that night disguised as Vishnu, she asked him to fulfil her mother's wish. In the guise of the god, Lohajangha said to his beloved "Your mother is a wicked old woman and I cannot take her to heaven in front of everyone. But the doors of heaven are open on the morning of the eleventh day and many of Shiva's *ganas* enter at that time, before anyone else. I can slip your mother in with them if she changes her appearance. Shave her head with a razor so that only five locks of hair are left and put a garland of skulls around her neck. Strip her of her clothes and cover her back with soot and her front with vermilion. Then she will look like a *gana* and I will be able to push her into heaven easily." Lohajangha stayed with Rupinika a little while longer and then he left.

'In the morning, Rupinika prepared her mother as she had been instructed and the old woman remained like that all day thinking about heaven. When Lohajangha arrived that night, Rupinika handed her mother over to him. He took the old woman, naked as she was and made-up as he had directed, climbed onto his bird and flew away. From the air, he saw a huge stone pillar with a disc on top of it in front of a temple. He set the old woman down on top of the pillar. She held onto the disc for support and swayed in the wind like a banner that announced her mistreatment of Lohajangha. "Stay here while I go and bless the world!" he said to her and disappeared.

'Lohajangha saw that a crowd of people had gathered in the temple courtyard to maintain an all-night vigil before the temple festival. Lohajangha addressed them from the sky. "Listen! Today, in this very place, the destructive goddess of smallpox shall fall upon you! Come, take refuge in Vishnu!" The people of Mathura were terrified when they heard this voice from the sky and begged for Vishnu's protection and prayed that the calamity should not befall them.

'Lohajangha came down from the sky, took off his godly disguise and slipped, unnoticed, into the crowd. Sitting on top of the pillar meanwhile, Makaradanshtra began to worry. "The god has not returned and I have not yet reached heaven!" she thought. She could not hold any longer and began to slip off the pillar. "I am falling! I am falling!" she cried and when the people below heard this, they became hysterical with fear, believing that the smallpox goddess was about to descend on them, just as they had been warned. They began to shout, "Goddess! Do not fall! Do not fall!" The old and the young in Mathura somehow managed to get through that long night, fearing each moment that the goddess would fall on their heads.

'When the night was finally over and morning came, they saw the old woman on top of the pillar in her wretched state. The people and even the king recognized her at once and they forgot their fear and burst into laughter. Soon Rupinika heard about the incident and came to the temple. When she saw that it was her mother who was on top of the pillar she was very embarrassed. She managed to bring her down with the help of the people gathered there. Everyone was dying of curiosity and asked Makaradanshtra what had happened to her. She told them the whole story.

'The king, the Brahmins and the merchants who were there were sure that all this had been the work of some magician or sorcerer. They announced that whoever had tricked the old woman should reveal himself and he would be honoured immediately. Lohajangha came forward and when he was questioned, he narrated the whole story, right from the beginning. He offered the gifts sent by Vibhishana to Vishnu and the people gazed at them in wonder and admiration. The citizens of Mathura honoured Lohajangha and by the order of the king, Rupinika was made a free woman. Now that Lohajangha had taken revenge on Makaradanshtra for all the troubles that he had to endure because of her, he lived happily in Mathura with his beloved Rupinika, rich with the jewels he had brought back from Lanka.'

Dushmanta and Shakuntala

Shovana Devi

In the days long, long gone by there was in India a great
primeval forest. In it were giant banyans, thick with aerial
roots like lion's manes; lofty, sky-scaling deodars; and rows
beyond count of tall sentinel-like palmyra trees. A little
silvery brook, the Malini, wound in and out amongst them,
and in the distance rose the encircling hills.

The waters of the Malini were still and unruffled, save
for an occasional ripple. Upon their tranquil surface, as in
a mirror, could be seen reflected the blossoming trees on its
banks, patches of blue sky peeping through them, golden
clouds, birds on the wing, and even the tops of hermits'
cottages rising amid the sacred groves surrounding them.

On either side of the Malini stretched miles and miles
of jungle, a paradise of wild beasts and birds. Wild geese,
with wings edged with gold, sported all day among its
golden lotuses; long-necked cranes, those birds of infinite
patience, would stand motionless for hours on one leg in its
shallow water, sly and demure, ready to dart on any
unfortunate little fish which might venture near them;

'Dushmanta and Shakuntala', from *Tales of the Gods of India* by
Shovana Devi. London, 1920.

while goldfinches and kingfishers wheeled about it at all hours. There were many species of smaller birds, too: swarms of mynas and parrots and parakeets, green as leaves, which sang in the sacred groves and built their nests under the eaves of the cottages. There frisked and bounded at pleasure little baby fawns away from their dams, now amidst the waving golden corn, now on the soft, grassy sward beside the cottages. In spring the koels sang among the flowers; in the rains the peacocks danced to the rumbling of the thundercloud.

On the bank of the Malini, beneath an ancient banyan, many centuries old, was the home of Father Kanva, a mighty sage. He wore long, matted locks gathered up into a knot on his head, and a white, reverend beard flowed down his aged breast. There lived with him his sister, Gautami, a holy matron of sweet temper and gentle disposition. Their cottage was of wattle and leaves, their dress of bark. There were glossy milchkine and restless calves in their cattle-pen; and there were also a few bark-clad hermit boys, pupils of Father Kanva.

These boys used to read the scriptures with him; they performed their sacred rites with the water of the Malini, and entertained his guests with the fruit of his trees and made offerings of woodland flowers to their deities. Daily they went to the wood to gather dry twigs and sticks for the sacred hearth-fire, and take their master's cattle, black and white and brown, out to graze. There were green pastures for the kine and calves, and cool shades where their guardians, the little hermit-boys, could play and rest. There were sands where the boys could build their castles, clay to make their birds, reeds and bamboos for their flutes, broad banyan leaves for their rafts or ships, little fawns in the wood and peacocks in the trees to be their playmates. In the twilight they would either sit round Mother Gautami to hear the old tales of the battles of the gods and demons, or join Father Kanva in the chanting of sweet Sham-Vedic hymns.

Thus they had everything to make glad their hearts, saving that lamp of beauty, the little laughing girl Shakuntala. She was soon to come like a beam of heavenly light into their home. One midnight, when all the hermitage slept, the nymph Menaka abandoned there her new-born child. Wild birds, Shakuntas, or vultures, covered the babe with their wings and guarded her from harm, the creatures of the wood thus showing her more love than her own flint-hearted nymph-mother!

Early in the morning the hermit boys went to the woods, as was their wont, to gather fruits and flowers. They had gathered amloki, haritoki and ingli fruits by the hundred, and had begun to pluck the wild flowers for offerings when, lo! they came upon the fairy babe guarded by the birds, lying among the flowers, herself a fairer flower. They picked her up and took her to Father Kanva. The Shakuntas, her guardians, followed her to the hermitage, and after her the little fawns ran frisking; and the birds, loath to part from their tender ward, built their nests in the aged banyan tree above, and the fawns lay down below to be her playmates. She was given the name of Shakuntala, after the birds who had kept watch over her through the night.

Under the broad shadow of the venerable banyan, in the fond care of Mother Gautami, Shakuntala grew to loveliness and womanhood; and in due time Father Kanva went abroad to seek a bridegroom for her, leaving her to show the hospitality of the hermitage during his absence.

Shakuntala's mother was the fair nymph Menaka, and her father none other than the greatest royal Sage, Vishvamitra; but their heartlessness made them utter strangers to her. She thought of Father Kanva as her father, and of Mother Gautami as her mother, and the hermit-pupils were her brothers; as for her kine and calves, they too shared her love, and even the wild plants and creepers about the hermitage were dear to her. She cherished two girlfriends, Anasuya and Pryamvada; but closest to her heart was a motherless baby fawn, as unquiet as a baby well could be.

The three girls were never idle. Besides the usual household work, they served the guests at the hermitage, watered the plants and creepers in their little garden-plots, and amused themselves by marrying mallika creepers to mango trees. Further, Anasuya and Pryamvada had set themselves an interesting task—daily by turns they had to water and watch a particular madhavi creeper, because they had vowed that Shakuntala's bridegroom was to come the very day the madhavi should flower.

After caring for the plants, which were almost as dear to them as their own sisters, the three friends would wander from wood to wood, gathering flowers, or would sit and chat and sing beneath the groves, murmuring like humming bees, or would swim and frolic swan-like in the crystal waters of the Malini. In the evening, when the sky wore crimson and gold, these little wood-nymphs would return to the hermitage.

Time passed, and lo! one day there came a soft vernal breeze, unfolding the golden buds of their beloved madhavi creeper. 'The madhavi has flowered,' said Anasuya and Pryamvada, jestingly, to Shakuntala. 'Thy bridegroom comes today.'

The king of the country was named Dushmanta, and there was no greater Prince than he. He was king over the East, the West, the North, the South, over all the seven seas and all the thirteen fabled rivers that encircle the Earth. He was sole Overlord of the World and King of Kings. He had unnumbered troops in his barracks, unnumbered elephants in his elephant-yards, countless horses in his stables, a myriad gold-and-silver carriages and chariots standing ready, and a host of serving-men and women in his golden palace, which spread for many a mile. A brahmin

youth, Madhavya, was his companion and bosom friend.
The name and fame of Dushmanta reached to the far ends
of the earth.

The very day the madhavi flowered the King of the
Seven Seas and Thirteen Rivers said to his friend
Madhavya: 'O Madhavya, let us go forth to hunt today.' The
brahmin shivered at the word 'hunt' as if he had the ague.
He lacked nothing at the palace, where he could get enough
cakes and sweets and milk and curd and honey to glut his
appetite, but the fear of having to contend with bears and
tigers in the woods almost took away his senses. He dared
not oppose the king, for brahmin though he was, it was not
in his power to dispute his wish. So there was much stir
and bustle: the elephants and horses were got ready, the
wrestlers girt up their loins; the shikaris came out, carrying
long spears; the fowlers came out with their bows and
arrows, the fishermen with their fishing nets and rods; and
last of all the charioteer of the king drove a golden chariot
up to the golden lion-crowned palace gate, which swung
open with a musical sound.

King Dushmanta went out to hunt in his golden
chariot. On either side of him walked two tuskers, fanning
him with chamars or chouris (bushy yak-tails). An officer
of rank held over his head the gem-handled royal umbrella,
fringed with pearls. The royal musicians went ahead,
beating drums of victory and proclaiming the event to all
and sundry, and last of all in the procession trotted
Madhavya on a limping mare.

The king drew one wood after another until at last the
hunt began. The fowlers set their bird-traps in every tree,
the fishermen cast their nets into every stream and lake,
the beaters surrounded the wood, and there was much
rushing to and fro of its panic-stricken denizens.

The birds flew in terror through the trees; their young
ones were fluttering their wings, green as leaves, and
peeping timidly through the foliage. Some of them hung to

the boughs by their legs like golden fruits, some sought
their nests in the hollows of the trees, while others kept
hopping from branch to branch, keeping up a loud and
terrified screaming, for the fowlers were busy with their
traps and snares. The wild buffalo were rolling over in the
mud or standing up to the horns in water in the heat of the
day; when they scented danger, they fled into the forest
with horns lowered in menace. The elephants were at their
bath, sprinkling water over their bodies through their
trunks; some of them stood rubbing themselves against the
shala trees while others were waving branches to and fro
about their flapping ears to drive off the flies and
mosquitoes. Suddenly they stood quiet a moment, listening,
with their trunks raised, then stampeded, bellowing aloud,
treading down the golden lotuses, tearing to shreds the nets
of the fishermen, spreading destruction wherever they
passed. The wood rang with the growls of the tigers; the
lions roared fiercely in their mountain-dens; the whole
forest was in commotion.

Many birds were caught in the traps, many pigs felt
the points of the spears, many tigers were pierced with the
arrows, many bears fell to the swords; a cry of mingled pain
and panic filled the wood. The unwounded tigers fled into
the thicker jungle; the fishes and crocodiles dived into the
deeper waters; the birds sought refuge in the heights of the
sky.

The fowlers pursued the birds with their traps, the
hunters pursued the tigers with arrows ready on the
bow-string, the fishermen pursued the fish with sweeping
nest, and the king in his golden chariot raced after a gazelle.
Away bounded the gazelle with long leaps, lightly
skimming the ground, the king pursuing with lightning
speed. The troops, the hunters, the horses, the elephants,
and even his dear friend Madhavya, all were left far behind.
Now by the winding stream, now through the heart of the
wood, now over field and meadow the king pursued the

panting deer.

While such scenes of cruelty made hideous the wood, all was quiet and peaceful about the hermitage of Father Kanva. The parrots in its sacred groves were busy splitting open ears of golden paddy with their ruby bills; the swans were floating majestically in the Malini; the fawns were frisking and bounding on the kusha grass beside the hermitage; and the three girl friends, Shakuntala, Anasuya and Pryamvada, were prattling sweetly beneath their madhavi bower.

Every creature in the hermitage was at ease and happy; within its sacred precincts none could think of harm and cruelty. The panther drank water at the Malini with the hind, and both lay down in the shade together, while the baby-fawns played with the lion-cubs—such was the hermitage of Father Kanva. The king's quarry, the gazelle, ran for her life into this sanctuary and stood beside Shakuntala, gasping and looking behind her in terror. The king threw down his bow and arrows, alighted from his golden hunting car and walked towards the hermitage to do reverence to the great sage. On the way he chanced to overhear a conversation between the three girls in their bower. A bee had just left a madhavi blossom and had begun buzzing round the rosy face of Shakuntala. 'O drive the bee away,' she cried to Pryamvada at her side.

'Call on King Dushmanta, the sole chastiser of the wicked,' said her friend, smiling. 'He will deliver thee from the dreadful bee.'

Dushmanta could have found no better time to present himself before the playmates. He rushed into the bower, saying: 'Ah! while King Dushmanta yet governs the world, how dares a bee molest the lovely daughters of the pious hermit?' In another moment the king had caught the bee. 'How wouldst thou have me punish this wicked bee, O large-eyed maiden?' he asked of Shakuntala, who blushed to the roots of her hair and pointed to a lotus floating in the

Malini. 'Ah! I understand thee,' said the king. 'I must imprison the bee within the petals of yonder lotus.' He made it captive in the flower and turned to Shakuntala, but she was too tongue-tied by maiden bashfulness to say a word of thanks to him, and the lilies of her cheeks were mingled with the rose.

Thus did the King of the Seven Seas and Thirteen Rivers meet the beauteous Shakuntala in the madhavi grove, and their lives were knit in love from that hour.

It is time to return to the king's companion, the young brahmin, Madhavya. He fancied himself every minute in danger of his life, and longed to return to the palace. He was used to delicate food, he slept on a soft downy bed, and never went out except in a sedan chair. What a contrast was his life in the jungle! All day he had to remain in the saddle, following the hunters; the cries of 'There runs a bear! There goes a tiger!' perpetually rousing his fears. For drink he had only the dirty water of the pools; for food he had to eat the half-roasted flesh of the game; and how could he sleep on a bed of leaves with the mosquitoes ever about his ears? He was famished and worn out, and his bones were well nigh shaken out of their joints. His long rides after the wild beasts made his limbs stiff and swollen with pain; and worse than all these sufferings was his terror of bears and tigers ready to spring on him from every bush. He was haunted by the dread of a bear catching him by the nape of the neck, or of a tiger snapping off his head as one breaks a piece of sugarcane.

At last Madhavya limped up to the king and said, 'I am hungry and weary, and my strength is gone from me. I can endure no longer.'

But his plaint was cut short by Vadrasena, the officer in charge of the king's hunting arrangements, who suddenly made his appearance. He found the king rather morose, so he began to dwell upon the pleasures of the chase. 'What pleasure, O king,' said Vadrasena, 'can equal that of the proud archer when his arrow strikes his flying quarry? How he delights in the chase, happy as he beholds his prey turning in rage or fear! Shall we not, then, push onward through the forest?'

Aching for the ease and fleshpots of the palace, Madhavya protested. 'O king,' the Brahmin cried, 'why should we linger in the wood? The kingdom suffers by thy absence, and thy health is menaced by such hardships. Pay no heed then to Vadrasena, who lives but for the chase, and let us all retrace our steps homeward.'

The king turned a deaf ear to both counsels; to be near Shakuntala was all he now desired, and he proposed to stay on at the hermitage like a king turned hermit, abandoning the hunt, and leaving his State to take care of itself. 'We are encamped hard by a sacred hermitage O Vadrasena,' said the king, 'where we do ill to celebrate the joys of taking life. Let the antelopes browse without fear, and my bow repose with slackened string.' Sooth to say, he had no longer the heart to shoot at those beautiful antelopes whose soft large eyes reminded him of his beloved Shakuntala.

However, since Madhavya could not bear the hardships of a forest life, that served as an excuse to send the brahmin home, together with the large hunting-party whose presence disturbed the peace of the hermitage. The whole party had soon withdrawn from the wood, leaving the king alone.

'Ah, now am I Prince regnant,' said Madhavya to the king as he left the wood, strutting like a peacock. 'I go in procession with my retinue, while not a fly is left behind to buzz about thee.'

Thus he returned to his old comforts at the palace and began to play the king, while the king himself wandered about the wood crying, 'Shakuntala! Shakuntala!' The bow had dropped from his hand, the arrows had fallen out of his quiver, the royal dress had become tattered, exposure to the sun had made swarthy his handsome complexion, and the king of the World had become a vagabond in the forest!

As for Shakuntala, she lay on a cool bed of soft lotuses in one or other of her favourite bowers by the Malini, sighing for her royal lover and writing love-messages on lotus leaves with her pearly nail. For she had lost her heart to the king, and at the thought that she might never see him again her breast would heave with sighs and her large eyes fill with tears. On either side of her sat her friends, Anasuya and Pryamvada, fanning her with lotus-leaves, wiping away her tears or consoling her, their arms thrown fondly round her neck, saying: 'O Shakuntala, the long dark night will soon be over for thee. The king will return to thee with the returning sun.'

The long night came to an end at last for Shakuntala. There was a gleam of golden light in her bower, a flutter of golden wings, and a stirring of the madhavi leaves. The lilies in the Malini spread out their golden petals to the sun, the birds broke forth into song, the fawns, her favourites, came frisking towards her, and then into her bower came her royal lover.

There the King of the World and the Queen of the Wood met and exchanged garlands. Anasuya and Pryamvada stood witnesses to the marriage, for this was the gandharva form of union, the privilege of princes.

The king dwelt with his bride at the hermitage until the time came for him to return to his realm. One golden evening he sped away in his golden chariot to his golden palace; and Shakuntala, weeping, was led back by her friends to the hermitage through the darkened wood. 'Stay, O Anasuya and Pryamvada,' cried Shakuntala, looking back after the king. 'My foot is hurt by this pointed blade of kusha grass, and my vest of bark has caught on a branch of the kuruvaka!'

With such pretences she thought to conceal her yearning for a last look at her departing lover.

So the king returned to his golden palace, and

Shakuntala went back to her wooden cottage and began to count the tedious days.

At the time of parting the king had presented Shankutala with a memorial ring engraved with his name, Dushmanta, saying: 'O beloved! count every day one letter of my name, and when thou hast counted out the last letter, a golden chariot shall come to fetch thee to my golden palace with befitting honours.'

All the letters of his name were counted over, and yet there came no golden chariot for Shakuntala. Day followed day and night followed night, and the golden letters of Dushmanta's name had been spelled out and counted over and over again, but still there returned not the golden chariot that had carried away her lover many, many golden evenings ago.

The King of the World was seated in splendour on his golden throne, and the Queen of the Wood crouched by her cottage door, lonely and brooding, well-nigh broken-hearted. Neglected were her guests, her pets, her bowers, even her bosom friends. There was no smile on her lips, no sparkle and lustre in her eyes. At night she lay tossing sleeplessly on her bed of leaves. By day she would sit motionless as a statue at her cottage door, looking anxiously towards the road for the coming of the royal chariot.

The months went by, and yet it came not. 'What!' she mused to herself, with a pang at her heart, 'has the king so soon forgotten his hermit-bride? Alas! how shall a forest blossom, a woodland beauty, hope to rival those garden flowers, his high-born palace dames?'

One day, while Shakuntala was sitting there, musing on her absent lover, with her lovely head buried in her arms, Durvasha, a master-curser, passed by and cried, 'Ho, there! give me alms!'

Shakuntala did not hear his words, for she was unconscious of his presence and rose not to welcome him.

Durvasha flew into a rage at her neglect of so mighty a guest as himself. He shook with passion and cursed her, saying: 'Thou hast failed to recognize thy guest before thee; so shall thy lover fail to recognize thee when next thou meetest him.'

Even this curse Shakuntala heard not, but it was heard by Pryamvada and Anasuya, who were gathering flowers near at hand. They ran to fall at his feet and intercede on behalf of their friend, who was still seated motionless, supporting her languid head with her left hand.

'The word of a sage cannot be recalled,' said Durvasha, relenting, 'but her lover shall recognize her when he sees his ring.'

Shakuntala had the ring, her lord's parting gift, on her finger, so her friends thought no more of the curse for the present. Yet it was because of this curse that the king forgot to send his golden chariot for her.

Durvasha went away, and Father Kanva returned to the hermitage soon after. He had wandered over the world in quest of a bridegroom for Shakuntala—but none could be found worthy of her hand. It was with thankfulness, therefore, that he learnt that Shakuntala was already married to Dushmanta, the Overlord of the World. He now made preparations to sent her to her royal husband, whom she was about to present with an heir.

Father Kanva embraced his daughter and blessed her. Shakuntala wept half in joy and half in sorrow. Father Kanva's love had made an oasis in the desert of her heart. She flung herself into his arms and wept, her head buried in his bosom.

Father Kanva consoled her and bade her take courage. He called her friends, Anasuya and Pryamvada, and asked them to help her to array herself befittingly, for she was to be sent to her royal husband. They took her hand and led her away, and put upon her a new robe of bark, scarlet as the dawn. Pryamvada wove her a keshora wreath, Anasuya fetched her scented oil, the essence of wild flowers. They dressed her hair and adorned it with amaranths; they put vermilion in the parting of her hair, the sign of a wedded wife; they painted red her feet, which glowed like lotus-blooms.

Thus on her body she wore tree-stems for bangles. On her neck she had a keshora garland for a chain; in her hair wild flowers took the place of jewelled combs—alas! what mean apparel for the Queen of the World! Anasuya and Pryamvada were not content, yet where could these poor daughters of the hermitage find pearls, or diamond bangles, or silken robes, or golden anklets for their friend?

Shakuntala was kind to the beasts and reverent to the nymphs of her woods, so they were all sad to lose her, and still more so to see her go thus, sorrily dressed. And lo! the silkworms wove her a rich silken robe; the oysters of the Malini offered her a chain of pearls; and the nymphs of the woods gave her jewels of every hue, beyond all price. Her graciousness had won her treasures to rejoice the heart of any princess.

Anasuya and Pryamvada hastened to help Shakuntala put on her wonderful array and, little as these simple girls could know of such splendours, Shakuntala soon stepped forth as fitted the bride of a king.

Now arrived the auspicious hour for her departure. She was loath to leave the peaceful hermitage, her woods and her pets, the little fawns and flowering creepers and plants, and the silver brook Malini, which formed part of her being. Still more unwilling was she to leave for ever her bosom friends, Anasuya and Pryamvada, without whom she knew not how she could live. The time had come to bid farewell to all her girlhood had known and loved. The young tender leaves of the jasmine and mallika creepers waved to and fro as if beckoning her back to them. Shakuntala went to them and, embracing a madhavi creeper whose crimson blossoms lit the grove, she said: 'O most radiant of twining plants! receive my embraces and return them with thy

clinging arms. Sweet friend, I am going far away from thee!'
She next took leave of the beloved Malini, on whose emerald
bank she had passed her childhood, saying a loving word to
every tree that grew about it.

Suddenly Shakuntala, whose feet faltered, loath to
leave the little brook, found herself held back by something
clinging to the skirts of her robe. She turned round,
exclaiming: 'Ah, what detains me?' It was a little
motherless fawn which had so often been fed by her loving
hand that it had caught her garment to hold her for a last
caress. She fondled and patted it and then said to it, with
tears in her eyes: 'Why dost thou weep for me, tender fawn?
Go back, my darling; alas! that we must part!'

The aged Kanva, whose eyes overflowed with tears,
now gave Shakuntala his last embrace and blessed her,
saying, 'Mayst thou ever retain the love of thine husband!
O Shakuntala, thou art the Queen of Dushmanta, the
Overlord of the World. Thou sharest, O my daughter, the
loftiest of earthly thrones. Be as kind to thy servants as
thou hast ever been to the beasts and birds of this
hermitage, and seek not thine own gratification, nor forget
the precious lessons of the forest. Whenever thou art weary
of the cares of princely state, seek again tranquillity in this
loved and consecrated grove.'

With these words of counsel and consolation, Kanva
gave her a parting embrace, and Shakuntala began to sob
and weep. 'Thy tears, O my child, ill befit the going of a
Queen!' said Kanva.

Shakuntala now for the last time went round the
peaceful groves and delightful haunts of her childhood, and
said: 'O all ye trees of this sacred wood, in which the sylvan
goddesses have their abode! Shakuntala has come to take
her leave of you—she who quenched not her own thirst until
you were watered, she who left ungathered your fresh
emerald leaves though she would fain have had your richest
to adorn her locks.'

Anasuya and Pryamvada threw their arms round Shakuntala and wept. The antelopes looked up sorrowfully at her; the peacocks stayed their dance; the very trees of the grove seemed to shed tears with their falling leaves.

Thus Shakuntala left the hermitage for the golden palace of her husband, in the company of Mother Gautami and two pupils of Father Kanva.

After she had left the hermitage Father Kanva wept in silence beneath the last tree on the outskirts of the hermitage until, checking his immoderate grief, he said to himself: 'Since the body is bound to part company with the soul some day, why should I grieve when the weaker bonds of outside relations are loosened or even broken?'

Shakuntala was attended on her way by delightful breezes. Pools of crystal water aflame with lotus-blooms refreshed her, and birds cheered her along with their sweet songs. But on the way it chanced that she descended into the clear waters of a wayside stream to bathe, and there she dropped the graven ring her lord had given her, and went on her journey unaware of her loss. Alas! the means of undoing Durvasha's curse was gone!

Stage by stage she travelled till at last she reached the golden palace of her husband, rising storey on storey, and spreading over many a mile. The palace had seven rows of buildings, one enclosing the other, with courtyards between, after the design of a lotus enfolding petals within petals. In the first *mahal* or division of this sevenfold palace was the audience-hall of Dushmanta, with pillars of gold upholding a golden dome. Beneath this golden dome there was his golden throne, and there his Ministers were busy dispensing justice.

In the second *mahal* was his temple, with walls of gold adorned with frescoes of birds in diamonds, fruits in pearls and leaves in emeralds, and in the midst of it was the sacred hearth-fire, burning day and night.

The third *mahal* was his guest-house, and there every

day a hundred thousand guests were entertained to costly viands on golden plates.

The fourth *mahal* was a ballroom, and on its varnished golden floor were dancing beauteous dames flashing with jewels, their anklets tinkling in sweet music with their measured paces, and their graceful movements reflected on the crystal walls.

The fifth *mahal* was a hall of music, and here all the varied instruments of the world were being played by skilful jewelled fingers, and strains of enchanting music thrilled the scented air.

In the sixth *mahal* were the inner or private apartments for royal ladies, and the seventh, with a large pleasure park beautifully laid out with shady trees and sparkling fountains, was the king's own abode.

In this *mahal* the king lay on a golden couch, surrounded by every treasure of beauty and of riches, forgetful through the curse of Durvasha of his hermit-bride. Into this *mahal* Shakuntala was conducted, veiled from head to foot, and, as she walked in, the strains of a tender, melancholy song came floating to her ears: 'How canst thou, sweet bee, ever fond of the mango blossom, desert the first object of thy love for the water-lily?'

'Who art thou, and whence dost thou come, O fair maid?' asked Dushmanta of the veiled one. 'Dost thou desire wealth or some other boon? Speak, and it shall be thine.'

'Dost thou not know me, O king?' said Shakuntala, unveiling her face. 'I am Shakuntala, foster-daughter of Father Kanva, and thy wedded Queen. How canst thou forget me so soon? I ask no wealth of thee, but come to claim thee as my husband.'

The king paused a while as if trying to recapture an elusive memory of her, then said: 'Thou art the daughter of a hermit, and I am the Overlord of the World. What a gulf divides us! Could we be joined in marriage even in a dream?

Ask for wealth or jewels, and nothing shall be denied thee, but seek not to be my Queen.'

The worst fears of Shakuntala were now realized. She burst into tears and said in fear and trembling: 'Canst thou forget me, O king? Surely thou wilt recall the flowering of our love. Dost thou not remember the bee which was buzzing about my face? I was asking my friend Pryamvada to drive it away, and she said, smiling: "Call on King Dushmanta, the sole chastiser of the wicked." And as she spoke thou didst appear and drive the bee away, exclaiming: "Ah, while king Dushmanta yet governs the world, how dares a bee molest the lovely daughters of the pious hermit?" Does this not linger in thy mind, O King?' asked Shakuntala, looking eagerly into his face for a sign of recognition.

The king said, 'Nay!'

'Let me recall another word of thine,' said Shakuntala, still more confused and surprised. 'One day, as we sat together beneath the madhavi bower on the bank of the Malini, a thirsty fawn approached me and thou gavest it water, saying: "Drink, little fawn, drink." It refused to drink from thy hand, but received the water eagerly from mine; and thou didst say, with a smile: "Ye are both foresters, so this fawn loves thee." Is that gone from thy mind?'

'I resemble a bee,' exclaimed the king, 'fluttering at the close of night over a blossom filled with dew. Thou art bright as a gem; none could forget thee if he beheld thee but once. Yet am I perplexed by thee, for my mind retains no memory of the face. Hast thou not something more tangible than honeyed words to stir my recollection?'

'Thou floutest honeyed words!' exclaimed Shakuntala, overcome with shame and indignation. 'Alas! the honey of thy words did win my trust whilst thy heart concealed the weapon that was to pierce mine. Thou gavest me a ring on the day of our parting, saying: "O my beloved! repeat each day one of the letters engraved on this gem; and when thou hast spelt the word Dushmanta, a golden chariot shall come to carry thee to my golden palace." Would it arouse thy memory, if I showed the ring?' But when she sought to display the ring, it was not on her finger. The last means of breaking the spell laid on her husband's memory was gone.

'O Mother! I am undone,' cried Shakuntala, and fell in a swoon, wounding her forehead and staining the golden floor with her purple blood.

Menaka, the stony-hearted nymph-mother of Shakuntala, was even then playing on the lyre in the hall of Indra. Suddenly, as though by her daughter's fall, the strings of the lyre were sundered, and she knew that danger threatened her child. Leaving the halls of heaven, she flew into the palace of Dushmanta, dazzling his eyes by the lustre of her beauty, and carried away Shakuntala in her arms. She left her at the hermitage of the patriarch Kashyapa, on Hemakunt, the golden peak of Himalaya, the abode of the apsaras; and there in due time Shakuntala was delivered of a Prince, bearing on its little palms the marks of empire.

King Dushmanta, his senses still obscured by the curse of Durvasha, was bewildered by what had happened, and could neither rest nor sleep for many a day. Time passed wearily until a wondrous chance dispelled the curse. Some fishermen were one day ordered to catch fish in the river Shachi for the royal household. They caught many fishes of varied colours and sizes; silver carps, moony pomfrets, snaky eels, golden grabs armed with pincers, and red lobsters by the score. The golden and silver fishes were all heaped up in baskets on the bank. At last it grew dark, the shades of evening fell over the sky, the river and the roads, and the fishermen departed with their booty. One of them, however, remained behind, and, whirling his net over his head for a last throw, cast it on the water. Dark as a cloud it covered the river from bank to bank, and a giant fish, the king of the fishes in the river, found itself entangled in the net. It was dragged on shore with great difficulty by the delighted fisherman, who cut it open then and there lest it should escape into the water—and behold! he found in its stomach a ring, bright with a large gem worth a king's ransom. He was offering it for sale in the market when he was caught by the king's officers and brought up before the king himself for punishment. The fisherman told the king how he had found the ring inside a fish, and the king took it and at once recognized it. The curse of Durvasha was broken, and the king's memory of Shakuntala revived as in a flash.

The fisherman was sent away with a large reward; but the king, realizing that he had spurned and rejected his beloved bride, lost all his happiness and was sunk in woe.

'Alas!' he cried, in the agony of his despair, 'what frenzy blotted out the memory of my love for the daughter of the sage? Events are foredoomed by Heaven. The peerless Shakuntala is my wedded wife, and I have cast her from me, I know not why.'

Tears veiled his eyes, and a cloud came over his senses. He cried 'Shakuntala!' and fell into a trance of melancholy. When the inmates of the palace spoke to him, the name of Shakuntala would fall from his lips; then he would sit silent with his head on his knees, his lips parched with the heat of his sighs, and his eyes fixed open for want of sleep.

He felt no joy, waking or dreaming; he took no interest in his State business. His crown was a burden to him, and his parks gave him no pleasure. The hall of song was silent, the ballroom no longer echoed to the measured steps of the bejewelled beauties of the court.

In the meantime the eternal feud between the gods and demons had broken out afresh, and Dushmanta's services were demanded by the King of Gods. He went up to heaven and inflicted a crushing blow on the demons. After a few days' sojourn in Heaven, Dushmanta left for his home on

Earth, loaded with celestial honours and garlanded with a wreath of mandar flowers from Paradise. The nymphs of Heaven engraved on the leaves of Kalpataru, the golden tree of wishes, the glorious deeds of Dushmanta.

Matali, the charioteer of Indra, conducted Dushmanta back in the flying car of his master over the celestial river Mandakini, the Milky Way. The chariot moved over clouds laden with showers, for his rolling wheels dispersed their crystal waters; the horse of Indra sparkled with lightning; the high mountain tops seemed level with the lowlands; the trees strained aloft their branchy shoulders, but seemed leafless; the rivers made bright lines, but their waters were lost to view; and lo! the globe of Earth itself seemed thrown upwards to him by some stupendous force.

Soon he was passing over Hemkunt, the mountain of the gandharvas, the celestial musicians, which forms a golden zone between the eastern and western Seas. Here was the hermitage of the patriarch Kashyapa. Here the air was balmy and pure, and here were rills to bathe in, dyed yellow with the golden dust of the lotus, and caves for meditation whose pebbles were flawless gems.

Dushmanta descended on this mountain to pay his homage to Sage Kashyapa, and beheld a boy pulling a lion's whelp towards him by the mane in rough play.

'Open thy mouth, lion's whelp,' the boy was calling, 'that I may count thy teeth.'

This boy was the son of Shakuntala, Sarvadamana, the All-subduing. He did what he pleased with the wild beasts of Hemkunt. Under the shade of a giant banyan he used to play, with all the birds and beasts for his playmates. His throne he would make of a giant python, coiled up in a hundred folds, and there he would sit, surrounded by his companions, the denizens of the wood. The snakes would join their hoods one to another and spread them out like a royal umbrella over his head. On either side of him would stand two elephants, fanning him with broad lotus-leaves.

The bear was his minister, the lion general, the tiger his guard, and the jackal his spy. The parrot was his bosom friend—how it amused him by telling funny stories and its adventures in the lands it had visited! Sarvadamana thus made himself the king of the beasts and birds. He was loved by all, and he feared none.

When Dushmanta alighted on this mountain, the boy was playing with the lion's whelp, which had been forcibly dragged from the breast of the lioness. Now he opened its mouth to count its teeth, now rode on its back as he would ride on a pony, or pulled it about by the mane in play.

'The lioness will eat thee up if thou release not her whelp,' the attendant shouted. 'Set free this young prince of wild beasts and I will give thee a prettier toy to play with.'

The boy immediately stretched out his hand for the toy, and the king, as he gazed upon it, was surprised to find the little palms glowing with the splendour of the lotus-bloom and bearing the marks of royalty.

The attendant ran back to the hermitage to get the toy and soon returned with a clay peacock, exclaiming, 'Look, Sarvadamana, at the beauty of this bird, Shakuntala-vanyam,'

'Shakuntala! Where is Mamma? Where is Mamma?' cried out the boy, looking eagerly around.

The surprise and delight of the king now knew no bounds. He cried to the boy, gathering him into his embrace, 'Now I know thee for my own.'

'No, Dushmanta is my father and not thou,' replied the boy, showing his white pearls of teeth, and struggling violently away from his arms.

At that moment Shakuntala herself appeared in search of her son, robed in mourning apparel, with her long hair twisted in a single braid and flowing down her back. 'O my husband! O my husband!' she exclaimed as she caught sight of Dushmanta, and fainted away with excess of joy as he rushed forward and caught her in his arms.

When she revived she wept mingled tears of joy and
sorrow, and, noticing on his finger the ring whose loss had
been the cause of all her troubles, she exclaimed:

'Ah! is that the fatal ring?'

'Yes,' said Dushmanta, 'by the miraculous recovery of
it my memory was restored. Take it back, my beloved.'

'No,' replied Shakuntala, 'keep it with thee lest I again
should lose it, and with it thy love.'

With the blessings of the sage Kashyapa, Dushmanta
returned with Shakuntala and their son Sarvadamana to
Pratisthan, his capital, and lived there happily for many a
year.

In due time they installed Sarvadamana on the throne
under the name of Bharata, after which India is still called
Bharatavarsha, or the land of Bharata, and themselves
returned to the hermitage of Father Kanva to pass the
evening of their lives in peace and tranquillity. Then
Shakuntala of the antelope's eyes rejoiced to find herself
back amidst the delightful scenes of her childhood, and to
dwell again among her beloved subjects, the creatures of
the wood.

Love Poems

Amaru

Man

1

The tenuous bamboo bridge spanning the double tide of the Malini has been carried away, and now my handsome is cut off from me upon an island. Has her father enough black millet? The rain continues. Each night I climb up the hill from which I can see the trembling light of the house of Sarmicha. It shines in the wet darkness like a glance through tears.

2

Her robe clung close to her body, and the tissue of it became transparent. I thank you, rain. You were, Sanabavi, as if you were naked. But, when the rainbow broke in flower, who warmed your little shivering breasts for you?

3

If I had the talent of Valmiki I would write a poem with my

'Love Poems' by Amaru extracted from 'Two Sanskrit Lyric Poets: Amaru and Mayura' in *Eastern Love* Vol. II, edited and translated by E. Powys Mathers. London, 1927.

lover as heroine. The first ten parts would be given over to the ten fingers of her hands, for they wove a veil in which I have wrapped up all my ancient loves. And I would consecrate the ten others to the ten nights we spent at Mabhahat.

4

'Pity!' she says, with bruised breasts and disordered hair. With eyes closed and legs still trembling, 'Finish!' she says. She says in a choked voice: 'It is enough!' And now her silence grows eternal. Is she dead or sleeping, is she meditating in delight on what has happened, or thinking of another?

5

My tender friend, my Sodara, returns to her dwelling at sunset; Narayani, the guardian of the temple, leaves me as soon as the star Asva is shining, and I sleep alone on my reed mat. Too seldom I dream Narayani has stayed, caressing me until the dawn.

6

I have seen you at your source, a child could have jumped over you, O river, a bunch of flowers deflected you. Here you are a wide flood, and might engulf this fine boat. Alas, Dayamati! My love for Dayamati!

7

She makes me a precise salute, and withdraws her little feet under her fringes. She looks attentively at the flowers painted upon her fan. If I venture to caress her gazelle, she starts to smooth the feathers of her painted parakeet. If I speak, she asks a question of one of her women. I find a thousand delights in her timidity.

8

When you used to make dolls out of wet leaves, they always cried however much you rocked them. And once I told you to put your doll out in the sunlight. You have played with my heart since then and I have wept. But in the end I remembered my own advice, and my tears are dry for ever.

9

This is the first time that the wind blows from the east, O Sadami, O precious crown, and brings me the sound of the temple bell of Anagari. Soon the five flowers of spring will be scenting my house, and you, the sixth, will bring me in your hair the odour of the reed mat on which you have wept all winter.

10

If I told my pain to the torrent, the torrent would halt for me. If I told it to the palm tree, the tree would bend down about me. But you pass singing, and do not even regard me. I will tell my pain to the torrent. If the torrent does not halt for me, at least its water will refresh my brow. I will tell my pain to the palm tree. If the palm tree does not bend down about me, at least it will shade my grief. Once more I have conquered shame and told you my suffering. You refuse me the water of your lips, the shade of your shadow.

11

Your hair climbs down about your shoulders, and the forest of Vishamadita shelters the gilded temple of Misrakesi.

12

A swan sought the silvered flowers of the kumuda on a pool at night, and was deceived by the reverberation of the stars in the crystal water. He pecked at the glittering reflection of the stars. At dawn he did not dare to eat the flowers of the sitopala, though they were white over all the pool. He was afraid that they were only stars. Do not go on telling me that you love me, Sarmicha.

13

No one has dared to speak of you to me since you went away. But I have said your name to the wind as he passed me, and to a certain man as he lay dying. If you are alive, O my mistress, the wind will some day meet you as he passes, and if you are dead, the dead man will tell you I have not forgotten.

14

My thirst has redoubled since first I drank her lips. Nor am I astonished. There was much salt in that kissing.

15

O Gayatri, your love is more inconstant than the reflection of a branch in the water of a lake with boats. The lake is a mirror again when the boats have gone, but your heart is suspicious still when you have pardoned me.

16

It matters little to me that I shall never behold the thousand gardens and intricate palaces of Hastinapura, since Maya, Illusion, in the likeness of Parvati, stays in my dwelling. It matters little to me that I shall never behold the smile of Siddhartha in the temple of Suddhodana, since the smile of Maya, his mother, is mine in the smile of Parvati. My joy is as unshakable as Meru mountain.

17

Since your husband has got to depart at dawn, listen to me carefully. He must not see your joy; you must weep, and keep him; you must tell him that you have not the courage to stay in a room his absence leaves most desolate; you must go out to see to his horse, and bid the servant saddle the fastest.

18

I told you that I knew how to make you happy. I said the very old words which put a woman's fears to sleep. Now your tears smile at me as a child smiles at a dream.

19

Birds in all the trees of my garden, will you be able to imprison my longing in your musical net? It breaks out towards my lover whom I have not seen for thirty days. My longing would hasten and make haste and beat against her perfumed breasts, against her scented voice. Hold it not back, good birds.

20

She put marguerites into her belt and their petals closed. 'Oh, what is happening?' she asked, and I replied: 'You looked at them with the darkness of your dark eyes and they thought it night.'

21

Why have you no pity for my love? The stars do not disdain the sea. They can admire themselves in it.

22

I was surprised that the nightingale singing in the little tree did not fly off when I came near it. I stretched out my arm and touched that flower of music, and it had a broken wing. I am still singing of your beauty, Dayamati.

23

That voyaging cloud now strands on the root of the moon and is broken in pieces. O you who shall some day sing this verse, seek to find why I sighed in writing it.

24

'I am no fool, and it is useless for you to lie to me. I see the marks of her kisses on your breast.' But I strain her violently against my heart, removing those marks of indiscretion, and her memory of them.

25

If so many birds sing in the trees of Kavinda, and if the flowers of Kavinda can never die, if clouds are not known in the sky of Kavinda, dear: you once crossed Kavinda.

26

'You lie in my heart,' you said, and I thought you commonplace. Now I send you a leaf of balm by Gayatri. Slip it between your tunic and your breasts so that the perfume reaches . . . me.

27

Do not speak. Your love words add nothing to my happiness. Do not speak any more. Sit in this sun-ray.

28

She has come in spite of the tempest. If you had seen the small rain, Matraya, falling from the tree flowers into her hair and, as if the thread of her pearls had broken, shining upon her breasts. . .

29

The snow of loneliness falls on my heart and shivers into white fruit blossom.

30

The forest held you prisoner, and the trunks of the trees were the bars of your cage, O dawn. The stream sang a more joyous song to you, dawn, and the mosses were softer. But you broke your cage with light, and went away. I think of

Mahadahi who loved me for a morning.

31

She is alive no more, and the flowers still appear. O Death, now that you have got this girl how can you find time to go on killing?

32

The peacocks cried at nightfall and have beaten their wings and departed. They carried away the last fires of the sun in their proud fans, and the last embers of our love, it seemed to us.

33

Perfumes of love and smiles of love, O glory of the sun and splendour of the starry night, as set in the balance against death you fulfil my desire no longer! Girls of Lanka, palm trees of Sartha, streams of Maraki, songs of the wind in the cherry trees of Kamala, I say good-bye.

Woman

34

See how his violence has dispersed my powder of sandal; I spread it with so much art upon my breasts! See how tired my lips are still, and how the down of the couch has been soiled beyond all cleansing, and this veil torn in pieces!

35

Whither are you running, O leaping stranger at the borders of this forest? Has love let fly you, fair boy-arrow, and do you hurtle towards the dwelling of your mistress? The ground rejects you as the tambourine rejects the ball. Are you drunken with immateriality, trying to catch yourself away from your body?

36

I shall go, I shall find a pretext for being away until the twilight. I shall go. As I want time to lick over my happiness, I shall take the long path that passes in front of the fountain, and there I shall tell my comrades that I walk out to see if my father's fields have suffered from the flood. O victorious Love, I shall go, O wild heart!

37

This is the Winter season of long sleep. I lie down on my couch at twilight and invoke Matha, the god of gilded dreams. I promise offerings and sacrifices and yet I hardly ever dream of Sri Hari. When the storm shakes the walls of my little house, I prefer to lie awake and listen, for the wind walking through the bamboos of my garden says Sri Hari.

38

'He sleeps, sleep now in your turn,' said my women, and they left me. Then, in a drunken fit of love, I brushed the cheek of my young bridegroom with my lips. I felt him tremble, and saw that he had only pretended. I was ashamed at the time, but soon I groaned with happiness.

39

I now abandon my body to the kisses of the water; soon to the kisses of the hours. O kisses of the hours, will you also leave a perfume of lustral water upon my spirit?

40

Sometimes you can be so fair, O day; O night, so desolate. Sometimes so sweet, O night; so torturing, O day. If 'he means never to come back, I wish you were both dead.

41

My father is away on business, and my mother has been out since this morning upon a visit to my invalid sister.

Night is falling and I am too young and afraid to stay alone.
Come in, O pleasant stranger.

42

As the branch bends beneath the weight of that bird, so I
bend beneath the weight of your love for me; but when you
leave me, I have not the branch's resilience. Yet what does
it matter, O bird? Go on singing. I had forgotten that your
song would soon cease and that I had not got it yet by heart.

43

She said over and over very tenderly: 'Come and see my
parakeet.' I followed her into the house, but her women
spied on us, and she said: 'My parakeet must be in the
garden.' He was not under the arbour, for the scent of the
jasmine was too strong there. He was not on the bank of
the runlet, for a little boy was cutting wood there. We found
him at last in a deserted pavilion, on a gilded sofa.

44

We are but three, yet we are four, for Love dances beside
us. Night has fallen, but the breasts of Narani are light for
us. The flowers have closed their petals, but the breath of
Priva, as she turns near us, is our refreshment. Araha! Let
us dance our most secret dances, let our feet pleasurably
bite this moss! Move the tress of hair hiding your throat, O
Narani! Priva, come nearer! Look upon our bodies, Love,
for we are Narani, Priva, and Domihi. We love, and not even
the calling of Night, couched in the forest, can pluck as
asunder. Night wishes our plaints to be added to his great
murmur, but, araha!, we will dance till the violet morn! Not
till then will we carry Priva to our dwelling and drink the
wine of her sweat. Araha! Araha! Your belly is like a pool
lashed by the storm, O Narani! Why are you already
dancing the last dance? And thou, Priva! Priva! O Night,
we come!

45

I write this letter by the sufficient moonlight. My friends have called me, but I preferred to stay in this room since it is full of you. I am still weeping. I looked into the garden, and the shadow of a leaf of the bamboo wrote out an unknown word on the blue sand. It may have been your name.

46

I take a long time in carefully giving a severe fold to my eyebrows, and know how to harden my looks. I am an expert in correcting smiles. When my companions rally me, I fasten an absolute silence upon myself. When my heart is like to break, I tighten my girdle. But the success of these things is in the hands of God.

47

O night, you have often come to me softly and covered my face when it was weeping. A nectar glistens in my cup this evening, and my lover lies upon my breast. Stay with me as long as you will tonight, O night.

48

This is a Hymn of The Wife of the Buddha: O first and fairest of all men, O moon-featured! Your voice is as sweet as the voice of Kalavinka, the bird whose singing maddened God! O My bright husband! O terror of the armies of the Sages! You were born in the heaven of gardens, eternally sonorous with bees! Great tree of learning, sweetest of saviours, O my husband! Your lips are as purple as the plum, your teeth like frost, your eyes are lotuses, your skin a rose! O redolent of flowers! O my fair season! O perfume in the chambers of the women better than jasmine. . . . O Kanthaka, rarest of horses, whither has he ridden you?

49

If you remember my kisses, say my name once very softly as you crush your mistress.

50

My blood is calling him but he does not come. That dawn does not rise for me. I said to myself that this is life, that this is the lotus-strewn way. O moon, is it your frozen rays that thus devour my breasts? O breeze of the evening, O freshness charged with garden scents, you burn me terribly. My sight is not what it was. I am going to die.

51

She teaches me all her secrets: that it is better to soak our cheek-betel in snow water, that the powdered root of lemon-grass brightens our teeth, that nothing is better than the juice of green strawberries to reaffirm our breasts; but not how to forget a door I wept outside all night.

Man and Woman

52

What is the weather like this morning?
> I do not know.

What? You have crossed the village and you do not know?
> The land is white with the sun, but I cannot tell
> whether the day be fine or not until I know if you
> are gay or sad.

53

My dear, my very dear, where are you going thus in the black night?
> I fly as upon wings to the place where he who is
> more beautiful than the day awaits me.

And are you not frightened to run alone, my dear, my very

dear?

    Love with his terrible arrows keeps me company.

54

Have the cocks sung yet?

    The night is still blue above us, and you may sleep.
I have not slept, my eyes were closed but pictures passed
beneath my lids.

    What did you see, dear lover?
A house white with jasmine under the palm trees of Rami,
and us there very happy.

55

A fig of delight!

    Where?
A fig of delight! You cannot see it.

    Then tell me where it is.
Between two branches.

    This way?
No.

    That way?
No, no.

    Higher? Lower?
Lower. But do not move!

    You pick it then.
I shall climb up.

    O miserable! Mother! Mother!
What is the matter, my child?

    Nothing. I nearly fell.
How warm a thing is a fig, Sandati!

56

I was looking for you.

    I have been here a long time.
I am sorry. One of my kids escaped.

    You need not lie. I saw you with Madadari.

I asked her if she had seen my kid.

> And you hunted for it together?

Yes.

> A long time?

Quite a long time.

> That explains why she is walking with such difficulty.

57

My mother is not up yet. If you wish me to give you that kiss, come through the hedge.

> My hands are already bleeding from the thorny branches. Where are you going?

To fetch my goats.

> Your goats?

They have not eaten since last night, and will enjoy the thorns and the thorny branches. I shall be scolded, but shall have had your kiss.

58

I fear to be too warm.

> My house is by the side of a river, freshness inhabits it.

People would see me if I went to your house, my friend.

> My house is in the forest, only the orchids will see you passing.

The orchid would tell the bee, and the bee the parakeet, and he tells everything.

> The orchids would be dumb for a long time with ecstasy after you passed.

My mother would see my hair unmade when I got back.

> In my mirror you can make your hair again. It will keep the shadow of your smile for ever.

I love you and have forgotten how to smile.

59

You can ask what you will of me. My husband is far away.

Alas, alas! I only love the smell of growing jasmine.

60

Those love-wetted eyes that shut and half open like the wings of a dove in lust, that say so eloquently all that passes, on whom thrice-fortunate will you fasten them?

On him who speak to me of my dear love.

Woman and Woman

61

What did he give you?

A tortoiseshell lyre, two flocks, and a silver mirror.

How little!

Rather how much! For he gave me pleasure also.

You are very young.

Is it my fault he only gave you a she-goat and a sour memory?

62

He has just left me for ever, but I am brave, and none shall notice my despair. I smile. I am smiling.

Your smile is as sad as the first dawn over a burned village.

63

The girls washing their clothes make such a wanton babbling that I cannot hear what you say. Come near. Sit on my bed. Now you were saying? . . . She knotted her arms about my neck, her breath to my breath, and her lips set to mine.

64

'Caress my breasts with your fingers, they are small and

you have neglected them. Enough! Now set your mouth just
there immediately. Oh, why have you delayed so long?' She
was stifling her cries in her friend's hair when there came
a knocking at the door, and a voice said: 'We are the
Washers of the Dead. They told us that someone had died
here.' 'Next door at Harivansa's, in the name of God, next
door! . . . No . . . wait . . .'

65

He has fifty flocks, his face is of the true plum oval, his body
is incomparable. When he rises from bathing in the dark
lake it is as the moon emerging from the night. You must
decide!

> You are in a hurry?

In a great hurry.

> Then tell him that he will have to content himself
> by playing with my hair.

Are you mad? Why should I tell him that?

> Because this morning Vajuna offered the same
> sum, and by a bawd not quite too ugly for me to
> play with.

66

Who is there?

> It is I, and I have been knocking for a long time.

What is your name?

> Mahadeva, and I know you recognised my voice.

I did, for I was dreaming of you.

And here I am.

> You shall not come in, my dream suffices me.

67

O Dayamati, you know everything. Why do youths not look
at me? I walk against the wind until my tunic clings to me,
but they cross and continue their way. What must I do to
show them I am old enough?

You must let them suppose you have been loved already.

How?

Passionately.

I do not mean that. I mean how can I get the youths to notice it?

One day they will see that you no longer walk against the wind, and have draped your tunic into concealing folds.

68

By the sixty paps of Bhavita, I tell you he deceived you with Narayani, and I surprised them. Yesterday he took hold of my breasts by guile. Do you hear that? He took hold of my breasts. Also he kissed me by force this morning and tore my lips.

You lie!

Look at these wounds.

I cannot believe my eyes. I must taste them, taste them. I must taste them.

69

How can you leave that passionate lover to murmur at your door? Alas, alas, he might as well be writing his charming lines upon the sand, since you teach them to your wanton parakeet for fun. The young man is rich, and we have need of money.

70

And you love him?

Indeed I do.

Do you not know that I also love?

I was afraid so. Now there are two of us to love him. Even if one of us dies he will have a mistress.

You? You die?

We never know.

O Sadahi, star of my day, have you not understood that it is you I love, and that I am jealous?

71

What did he do then?
> He set a pillow of fresh grass under my head and went to fetch the milk.

And you slept?
> You are foolish. I rose and broke a branch of dadali and reddened my lips with the sap, I made my lids blue with the juice of the wild plum, I powdered my breasts with the pollen of the giant lotus.

Observation

72

He came to tell her that he was leaving her and that he loved another. She wept. He had departed, saying nothing of her new way of doing her hair.

73

She used to pass singing, but since that very handsome boy caressed her, she does not sing, and all is sad on the road she used to take. Why, Madahi, are you so desolate? Is there only one very handsome boy between the Red Mountain and the seashore?

74

He covered her face and her breasts and her arms with kisses, and then went away. Because he did not dare to kiss her mouth, she is passing her lips along her trembling arms now.

75

A gust of wind will blow open the petals of a poppy that is

slow in blossoming. Love suddenly brings the spirit of a girl to flower.

76

One day young Sita of Ratnavali indented this determination upon a rose petal: *The prettiest boy in all the world. But I will never love him. Love is too cruel.* She had just graved the last word when the West Wind carried away the petal.

77

'Clumsy!' said Narati. 'A fool!' said Dayamati, and they both laughed. But Ambati does not tell them that he has the most extraordinary eyes in all the world, and that the blackbird tries to peck at his mouth when he lies sleeping in the garden.

78

See how these vernal airs, charged with the sunrise water-lily, clear the bright sweat from the forehead of this girl, and tangle her hair, and swell her veil in the fashion of a lover, and give back her strength.

79

I have come out of doors the better to hear this passionate voice, which is kissing all the fields. It is of a woman, a warm and serious voice, saturate with love; but it has ceased. The nightingales have been dumb tonight.

80

. . . and those women who have broken their lutes go to dream by the small waters. . .

81

This dancer pleases you, but there are fifteen coveting her. Therefore carelessly drop an incendiary phrase into the conversation, say that the talent of the poet Sadasa is open to discussion, or that the army of Kamatrasnu is not

invincible. Let it work upon heated nerves, and the walls
will soon be shaking. Do not wait until your companions
come to blows, but make a sign to the dancer.

82

He entered the house of his mistress after long journeys,
trembling with desire, emotion and impatience. And he
found her surrounded by women friends, who took
malicious pleasure in prolonging their visit. But she was
more eager still, and crying: 'Ah, something bites me!' lifted
her veil and fanned out the flame of the only torch with it.
So that the guests departed.

83

As men speak:

You are imbecile to groan so because she has refused
to let you in. Wash away your tears and crown yourself with
jasmine petals. Sing one of the native songs of her servant,
for the girl is charming, more beautiful than Vadiha. She
will come out at once, and pay you for the rigours of her
mistress.

Leave me alone, for I love Vadiha! Leave
me alone!
The servant is very beautiful.
Beauty is not enough.
Her breasts, her legs.
Where does she come from?
From Mahapura.
Perhaps she knows my brother, who lives near
there. I will sing and bring her out, since you
advise it.
I am glad to see you love your brother so. Good-bye.

84

She remembers the dusk when he swore under the
flowering plum tree he would love her. She remembers his

betrayal, his lying, his brutal departure, and rejoices that she has escaped from such a man. But she never sees, save dimly, a branch of the plum tree flowering against the moon.

85

The chariot of the thunder is crashing over the clouds, it is almost quite dark and here is the rain! Come and take shelter under my tree, pretty. I invite you for the sake of your new tunic and for the sake of this bird in the branches of my tree. He has never seen a man and a girl not take advantage of a storm.' 'Alas, alas, I really must accept your invitation.' But even so the bird soon flew away.

86

Instead of the deep blue lotus her glance to him, her teeth in a lighted smile instead of the jasmine, instead of the cup one moving breast of hers. Thus, though she has little means, she finds a celebration for his return.

87

The gold band of princes is about his brow, he has thirty elephants and a hundred servants, his palace is on the bank of the Chandana, and he weeps tonight. He weeps as a labourer in a rice-field, who sees his crop borne down by the flood of the river. O master of thirty elephants and a hundred servants, you will not frighten Love. Your arrows and cutting-wheels will not frighten Love. So weep.

88

'Now may Love break my heart in a hundred and fifty-two pieces, put out the fire of my eyes, render me as thin as a harp, if I value that faithless boy more than a last year's nail-paring!' And then she cast an impatient glance along his usual footpath.

89

'You are more beautiful with no veils,' and he sets an impatient hand upon her girdle. Light grows in the eyes of the young girl, and her women file forth discreetly.

90

She is young, and has come to sit sadly under a certain cinnamon apple and regard the moon. Her breast is filled with sighs, she falls to weeping and then gives way to sleep. But the wind has listened and makes the cinnamon apple cry down its flowers upon her cheek, so that she dreams that a hand is wiping away her tears.

91

Bhavani, Ambalika and Rohini mirrored their smiling faces in the water. And Bhavani, crying: 'Oh, I am thirsty,' leaned over the gold disk which was the face of Rohini and kissed it as it floated trembling. And Ambalika must weep.

92

She looks at the torrent from the mountain where her lover keeps his flock, and says: 'Oh, have you seen him, torrent?' But the torrent answers with its spumy mouths: 'I have seen the blue sky and the white cliffs.' 'Have you heard the music of a bone flute, O torrent?' 'I have heard the noise of the wind breaking against the rocks.' 'O torrent, have you seen an eagle towering?' 'I have seen an eagle.' 'I am happy, torrent, for you have seen an eagle that saw Sadatta.'

93

O Fire, most mighty except for Indra, O fever of nature! Spilling from the snow mountains, flowing from the stars in shiny circles, Agni, Agni, Agni! You flicker, a thousand lotuses; you twist up iron like rushes; you flame in the heart of dancers, in the blood of gazelles gasping ahead of the hunt, in the arms of clinging lovers! Agni, Agni, Agni!

94

Her husband committed a small fault, and she recalled the eternal perfidious counsel of her women. She bore herself violently, thinking to frighten him; but he only remembered the unchanging sweetness of a certain girl.

95

The temple bell has let loose its arrow of sound upon the night, and rapid shadows are passing. That, by the sound of her silver bracelets, is Pritha. And that is Hatanena of the sad hair. That is Uma, and that is Gautami. Soon they will come back, each with a consecrated coal in a leaf of nenuphar; and as ever, because she sets it down in the grass to let herself be kissed, the dew will have quenched Pritha's.

96

Bhavani and Pritha are whispering. What are they saying? Now Pritha runs away. Where is she going? The little bell noises of her bracelets can be heard no longer. Far down there, see, two girls are scratching each other's faces, and a young man strips the petals from a flower.

97

Flutes becoming silent, young girls running, broken lilies. A storm.

98

How should we quench love when there is fire even in the pollen of the lotus under water, even in wet sandal essence, even in the dew of the frozen lantern of the moon?

99

She played with her collar of shells. She spoke to us of flowers, and her hands were as unsubstantial as a rose petal. She spoke to us of birds, and her voice saddened us

more than the crying of a lost bird at night. She spoke of
the sun, and her great eyes which had been suns were
dimmed to two thin sparks, eaten by the shadow.

100

O Death with the face of Dawn! O flower-
crowned Death! O drunken with having held
the bodies of every man and every woman in
your arms since time began! Death with
sealed lips! O Death, deaf to the supplication

of the fallen dancers! Charitable to the
calling of the Buddhas! Crea-
tive Annihilation! Death
with the face of
Dawn!

Pururava and Urvashi
(Epic version—Mahabharata)

Shovana Devi

Urvashi, daughter of the Sea-foam, was the fairest among the nymphs of Heaven, not excepting even Menaka, nymph-mother of Shakuntala. Exiled by the twin gods Mitra and Varuna, the Day-sky and the Night-sky, Urvashi had to leave Heaven and dwell for a time on Earth. Sadly she roamed the world without a companion save her two pet rams. One day, in the course of her wanderings, she met Pururava, son of Budha, and Pururava became enamoured of her celestial beauty.

'O fair one,' he cried, 'I look upon thee with eyes of love. Be thou my bride.'

'Only on two conditions can I wed thee,' said Urvashi. 'First, I must have these two rams always with me; and second, never must I see thee otherwise than fully clothed.'

To these terms Pururava agreed, and Urvashi became his bride.

All the nymphs and fairies mourned the loss of their Queen, and Heaven was joyless in her absence, so her

'Pururava and Urvashi', from *Tales of the Gods of India* by Shovana Devi. London, 1920.

friends the gandharvas, or elves, came stealthily into her room one dark, cloudy night, and carried off her rams. Urvashi cried out for help, and Pururava, forgetful of his vow, rushed into her room, not waiting to put on his garments, but could not see the robbers in the dark. Suddenly there was a flash of lightning, and Urvashi saw Pururava there unclad. Thus the conditions were broken, and Urvashi returned to her home in Heaven and made the gods happy once more with her dances and songs.

The Hero and the Nymph
(Classical version—Kalidasa)

Shovana Devi

Once upon a time there reigned over Pratisthana a demigod named Pururava. He claimed the golden Sun and silver Moon for his ancestors. Ila, daughter of the Sun, was his mother, and Budha, son of the Moon, was his father. Oft-times had he visited the Sun and Moon gods in Heaven in his golden chariot.

On one occasion, while returning to Earth from a visit to the Sun god, he chanced to hear some apsaras or nymphs crying out for help. Instantly Pururava turned his car in the direction of the cry, and found that it had come from a band of nymphs on Hemkunt, 'the golden peak of Himalaya'. As he neared the mountain, the nymphs cried out to him: 'O Pururava, a demon has carried off Urvashi, Heaven's fairest nymph. Often hast thou warred on the side of Indra, King of Heaven, against the demons. Now rescue his hapless nymph.'

'Wait on this golden peak, fair nymphs,' said Pururava, and shot away with lightning speed through the air in

'The Hero and the Nymph', from *Tales of the Gods of India* by Shovana Devi. London, 1920.

pursuit of the demon, scattering the clouds before him. Soaring and swooping, even as an eagle flies after its quarry, he overtook him at length, and there was a fight between the Demigod and the demon, and the struggle swayed this way and that, until at last Pururava succeeded in putting his enemy to flight and rescuing Urvashi.

Urvashi had fainted away, and looked more beautiful than ever in the swoon. In the twinkling of an eye Pururava returned with his lovely burden to the golden peak, and as he was descending Urvashi was thrown right into his arms by a sudden but happy movement of the car. She came to herself, and Pururava said to her, 'Behold, O nymph, thy friend and deliverer, Pururava.' She looked up into his face, and her bright, adoring eyes met those of Pururava, and told a tale of love and gratitude.

As the car landed on the peak the nymphs pressed forward with extended arms to embrace Urvashi, crying out in chorus, 'Eternal be the power of Pururava!'

Scarcely had the echo of the greeting died away when lo! another car, flaming up half the Heavens, alighted on the peak. 'Welcome, O King of elves and fairies!' exclaimed Pururava. It was Chitra Ratha, the charioteer of Indra, King of the gods, sent down to bring Urvashi back to Heaven.

'O Pururava,' said Chitra Ratha, 'well hast thou served Indra by rescuing the fairest of his nymphs. With everlasting glory thou hast crowned thy name.'

'O Chitra Ratha, I am but his humble tool,' replied Pururava. 'The glory is his, not mine. If the echo of a lion's roar frightens away an elephant, it is the lion, not the echo, that deserves the praise.'

'Humility is ever the ornament of valour,' said Chitra Ratha to the brave Pururava, and prepared to depart. As their flight began Urvashi cried out: 'O Chitra Ratha, wait! My golden chain is entangled with this straggling vine.' This was but a pretext, for she longed only for one last look behind at her deliverer, Pururava.

'The cruel nymph has borne away my heart in triumph,' said Pururava to himself after her departure. Despondency clouded his spirit as the days dragged by and brought her no more, and his yearning for the sight of her began to mar his happiness.

Spring came round with its wealth of flowers and song. The glories of the season lured Pururava from gloomy nooks and corners into his park, bright with a thousand flowers. The jasmine bowers were aglow with pearly blossoms, and the gilded bees swarmed about them, humming. The crimson creepers hung from every bough, waving to and fro gaily in the breeze. The koels, the soft, voluptuous breezes, the fragrant flowers, all these inflamed the soul of Pururava with love, but far, far beyond his reach was his Urvashi.

He said to himself with a sigh, 'The birds sing and mate, the fields are freshened, and the trees are decked with bloom, but there is no Spring for me without my love.'

Lo! as though in answer, Pururava heard above him a soft rustle, as of the fluttering of an autumn leaf. He looked up and beheld Urvashi on her way through the air to the Paradise of Mahadeva to act the part of Lakshmi in the play of Lakshmi's svayamvara (choice of a husband).

There was no time for more, so Urvashi threw down towards Pururava a vurja leaf. Pururava at first leaped back, thinking it to be a snake, and great was his joy when he found out his mistake. He picked the leaf up with tremulous fingers, and lo! it was a love-epistle from her, his beloved Urvashi. 'O Pururava,' thus it ran, 'I love thee. No more does my soft couch of flowers give me sleep at night, or the balmy breezes of Heaven bring peace to my love-tormented heart.—Urvashi.'

Pururava soon blotted out with kisses and tears the delicate characters traced by her tender hand on the leaf, but time went on, and still he saw her no more. He was sitting alone, one evening, on the terrace of his palace, sad at heart, when all at once light seemed to spread over the sky, and he looked up and beheld the rising moon at the gateway of the east.

He breathed a prayer to his ancestor, the Moon god: 'All hail to thee, O Moon, whose silvery beam dispels the gloom of eve. Canst thou not dispel the gloom within my heart?'

Even as he said this he heard the gentle music of anklets near him and felt soft fingers veil his eyes from behind. 'Thou art Urvashi, thou art Urvashi!' he exclaimed with joy, and turned to meet the embrace of his beloved.

'O King,' said the nymph, 'the Fates have at last brought me to thine arms. At the mansion of Mahadeva was enacted the drama of Lakshmi's choice of a lord. I played Lakshimi, and the nymph Menaka was Varuni, wife of the King of the Waters. All the gods appeared, headed by the radiant Purushottam (Vishnu, the Preserver). Menaka as Varuni had to ask me, "O Lakshmi, confess to whom inclines thine heart?" and I lost myself in that impassioned passage. I should have said—"To Purushottam," but, instead of that, "To Pururava!" escaped my lips. Unluckily thus I stumbled in my part and displeased Lakshmi. And so behold me, condemned to abide a time on Earth. Alas!' she added with a sigh, 'our faculties are but the slaves of Destiny.'

They were married by the gandharva rite, the exchange of garlands, the rite befitting heroes. 'O Moon,' they said together, 'and O Rohini, his beloved! Resplendent pair! hearken and bear witness to our sacred vows of love!'

Then Pururava and his nymph-bride betook themselves to the storied wood of Akalush, and by its silvery brooks, beneath the shade of its rich groves, passed many a happy hour. Together they would ramble through the blossoming woods and gather flowers and delight each other with songs.

But one day, as they roamed along the emerald bank of a stream, Urvashi stole away from her husband's side and entered a park forbidden to her sex, the park of the unwedded god, Kartick, the commander of the army of the gods. As a punishment, she was immediately turned into a vine.

Pururava looked around and about him for Urvashi, but found her not. He cried aloud, 'Urvashi! Urvashi! where art thou?' No answer came but the echo of his call. Frantic with sorrow, he rushed through the wood in search of his lost bride, nor desisted from the quest by night or day.

Once he looked up towards the Heavens and beheld a dark cloud fraught with lightning. 'Ah! thou dark fiend, thou hast stolen my beauteous bride,' he cried, mistaking the cloud for a demon and the lightning for Urvashi. 'I will slay thee, O felon demon!' With that he shot an arrow at the cloud, but it poured down cooling showers upon him and dazzled his eyes with flashes of lightning. He laughed wildly to himself, saying, 'This is no demon, but a friendly cloud. Refreshing raindrops fall, not deadly arrows, and I mistook the lightning for my love Urvashi.'

He pressed onward till he beheld a peacock, with neck outstretched and tail outspread, perched on a jutting crag. He made appeal to it: 'O bird of rainbow splendour, hast thou seen my beloved Urvashi? Tell me if, soaring skyward on thy wings, thou hast seen my nymph-bride in wood, meadow or dale? Thou canst not fail to know her by her large, soft eyes and her graceful gait.' But the peacock began to strut about and gave no answer.

'Ah!' exclaimed Pururava, reproachfully, 'thou wouldst be ashamed to show thy paltry plumage before the flowing tresses of my Urvashi. She is far away, so for a time thou mayest dance without a peer.'

He hastened on and next met a koel rending the air with its love-cries, and said, 'O nursling of a stranger's nest, hast thou chanced to behold my beloved Urvashi amidst these groves, warbling to herself melodious strains sweeter than thine own?' But the koel flew away, unheeding. 'Thou, too, O bird of tuneful song, desertest me like my beloved,' cried Pururava sorrowfully.

Pururava continued his quest, and at last heard a sound as of tinkling anklets like to Urvashi's; it was the plaintive note of migrating swans. He addressed the leader of the flock: 'Forbear awhile the course and hear my suit, O golden-winged Swan! Hast thou, by chance, on thy far wanderings beheld my fair Urvashi? Thou hast some tidings of my love; thy motions have a grace thou hast surely stolen from her. Know me to be King Pururava, the punisher of theives.' Away flew the swan with his flock as if frightened by a threat.

He next saw a chakravaka, or ruddy goose, playing hide-and-seek in a pond with its mate. 'Thou mayest measure my affliction,' said Pururava to the drake, 'by what thou feelest, if, but for a moment, thy fair companion hides in sport behind a lotus leaf. Say then truly, hast thou seen my beloved Urvashi?' The chakravaka answered not, but dived in the water.

Pururava went away, lamenting: 'Alas! Alas! the luckless have no friends.' He next turned to a swarm of gilded bees murmuring amidst the petals of a lotus, and said, 'O plunderers of the honeyed dew, have ye beheld my beloved Urvashi? It is folly to ask; ye would have sought her lips and not this lotus. Let me seek for her elsewhere.'

He went deeper into the wood and there found an elephant standing against a kadamva tree, and said to him, 'O King of the Forest, whose sports have felled the stateliest trees, know me to be thine equal. The golden Sun and silver Moon, these two, are my progenitors. Their grandson am I, and the chosen lord of the Earth and of Urvashi. Say then, hast thou by chance beheld my wandering bride? She is more bright than the Moon, her voice is more sweet than the sweetest note of music, and her glowing tresses wear the golden hue of the jasmine.' For answer the elephant trumpeted as if to say: 'Get thee hence and let me have peace in my forest.'

More melancholy than ever, Pururava journeyed on until he came to a grotto on the mountain side. 'Ay, such places are ever haunts of the nymphs of earth and air,' said he to himself. 'Perchance my Urvashi lurks within this grotto.' He looked in, then cried out: 'Ah! no, it cannot be, or the cave would be lit up by the lustre of her beauty. O Monarch of Hills, from whose hoary brows the streams rush down, hast thou seen a nymph daring with slender frame thy rocks and chasms, or resting in thy crowning woods?' But the mountain rolled back the words to him in mockery.

Thus flouted and ridiculed, he repaired to the bank of a silvery stream. 'What fond imaginings possess my soul as I look on thee!' said Pururava. 'Thy rippling wave is like to the arching brow of my fair Urvashi. Thy foamy spray is her white, loose, floating vest, and the flow of the waters her undulating gait. Thou art indeed my Urvashi, my lost Urvashi! Relent and return to mine arms.' But the stream flowed on oceanward, unmindful of his words.

'Thou art not my Urvashi,' cried Pururava, 'or thou wouldst not quit me even for the Ocean King.'

Hastening onward, he came to where a black buck lay reclining. Pururava addressed him: 'O deer of the soft dark eye, hast thou seen my fair Urvashi whose eyes rival thine own? O tell me if, wandering through the tangled maze of this wood, she has enchanted thy gaze?' But the buck sprang forward to join his mate and made no reply.

Thus mortally disappointed, the King wandered on and on like one possessed, until he came near a rock, through the cleft of which something sent forth a ray of light. 'Ah! that is my beloved Urvashi,' cried Pururava, bending down to see if it was she. It was no Urvashi, but a ruby more roseate than the blush of the Ashoka blossom. He picked up the ruby and said to it, 'O glowing gem! a ruby always brings luck to its owner. Be thou for me the Ruby of Reunion and restore to me my love.'

With the gem in his hand Pururava chanced upon the park of Kartick and there beheld a vine. 'What strange emotions stir my heart as I approach thee, O vine!' he exclaimed. 'No blossoms deck thy boughs, no bees court thee with their songs. And yet, O mournful creeper, there clings about thee something of the grace of my slender Urvashi.' He clasped the vine, saying, 'O vine of the wilderness, behold in me a long, heart-broken wretch. Thou art surely my love, and should relenting Fate restore thee to these fond arms, never more will I return to this unfriendly wood.' And behold! through the poser of the Ruby of Reunion, the creeper at once became transformed to Urvashi. She fell fainting in his arms, and Pururava caught her to his heart.

Soma and Tara

Shovana Devi

Tara, the star, was betrothed to Soma, the Moon god, already the husband of the twenty-seven daughters of the demiurge Dakshya. Despite her betrothal to Soma, Tara was married to Vrihaspati, son of a solar deity and preceptor of the Gods. He is now said to be the deity presiding over the planet of the same name, Vrihaspati or Jupiter.

The marriage, however, did not prove a happy one for Vrihaspati, for his newly-wed bride in her secret heart loved Soma and so suffered herself to be carried off by him.

There was great commotion in Heaven. There was much rushing and a great fight rushing to and fro among the gods, and a great fight ensued for the recovery of Tara. The gods were divided into two hostile camps. Some of them, headed by Indra, King of Heaven, fought against Soma, whilst others took his side in this battle for a bride. At this stage Brahma intervened, and at his request Soma released Tara.

Samudra or Ocean, father of Soma (for did he not arise from the churning of the Sea of Milk?), was wroth with him

'Soma and Tara', from *Tales of the Gods of India* by Shovana Devi. London, 1920.

for his abduction of Tara. He expelled him from Heaven and placed him among the stars by way of degradation. To this day Soma bears in the dark spots on his bright body the indelible stigma of his crime.

Samvarana and Tapati

Shovana Devi

Tapati, the Burning One, was another Sun-maiden, who burned, as the name implies, with excess of beauty.

For a long time the Sun god, her father, could find no fit mate for her, and this caused him perplexity and grief.

At that time there lived on Earth a votary of the Sun god himself, a certain King Samvarana. Samvarana was much given to the chase, and paid no heed to dalliance. 'Hunting he loved, but love he laughed to scorn.' One day, as he was out hunting deer on the mountains, he rode after a splendid stag, chasing him over hills and through valleys until his horse dropped dead from sheer exhaustion before he could overtake the stag. Undaunted, the king followed up the game on foot, and tracked it at last to a grove. There, instead of the stag, he found a charming maiden. Her golden hair wantoned with the breeze, and her beauty had all the splendour of the lotus blossom and was spotless as the crescent moon. The flowers and creepers in the grove caught the reflection of her radiant loveliness and seemed transformed into gold. She was Tapati, daughter of Surya, the Sun god.

'Samvarana and Tapati', from *Tales of the Gods of India* by Shovana Devi. London, 1920.

The King straightaway fell in love with her and cried out as he beheld her: 'O large-eyed maiden, who art thou? Surely a goddess, a dryad of the wood, or the Queen of elves and fairies, for no mortal woman could own such dazzling beauty. Whoever thou art, O fair one, be my bride!'

'I am the daughter of the Sun god, and my name is Tapati,' replied the maiden, blushing so rosily that for a moment Samvarana's eyes fell before her resplendent beauty. He rubbed his eyes and looked again, and lo! she was gone! The King fell to the earth in a swoon.

When he came to, he dedicated himself to the worship of the Sun god. For twelve days without ceasing he did him worship, and the god, pleased with his devotion, at last bestowed upon him his daughter. Long and happily did Samvarana dwell with his bride, the Sun-maiden.

The Ashvins and Surya

Shovana Devi

Surya, the Sun-maiden, was a young nymph of dazzling beauty, as a daughter of the Sun god well might be. She was betrothed by her father to Soma, the Moon god, or, some say, to his namesake, Soma the Vine, the Indian Bacchus. Nevertheless, all the gods were in love with her likewise, and all of them desired her hand, so wondrous were her charms even among goddesses. There was rivalry in Heaven over this Child of Light.

'Let us run a race,' said the gods at last, 'and as a prize the winner shall have her for a bride.' So it was agreed that they should run a race for her hand.

Indra, Lord of Heaven, Soma, the Moon god, Agni, God of Fire, Varuna, King of the Waters, Yama, Lord of the Dead, Vayu, God of the Winds, Kubera, God of Gold, and the brothers Ashvins all joined in the race. They started together, but were soon left far behind by the fleet-footed Ashvins, whom neither arrow nor steed could outstrip. The brothers Ashvins won the race and carried off the Sun-maiden in triumph in a golden chariot.

'The Ashvins and Surya', from *Tales of the Gods of India* by Shovana Devi. London, 1920.

Damayanti and Her Divine Suitors

Shovana Devi

Once upon a time there reigned at Vidarva a famous King named Bhima the Terrible. His chief title to fame was that he had an exquisite daughter named Damayanti. This Princess was waited upon day and night by a band of handmaids of surpassing beauty, but she shone among them like the moon among the stars, and her hand was sought, it is said, by both gods and mortals.

Nala, King of Nishada, came to hear of Damayanti's beauty, and was struck with passion for her. One day while he was seated in a grove, musing upon the beauteous maiden, he saw a flock of swans, with wings all flecked with gold, alight and begin to disport themselves close by him. Nala crept up to the leader of the flock and seized him. 'O mighty king,' said the swan, 'set me free, and I will do thy bidding, whatever it be.'

'If a bird can do a mortal any service,' replied Nala, 'fly to my love, Damayanti, O bird of golden wings, and tell her how much I love her.' With that he released the bird, and away it flew to Vidarva, rejoicing.

When the bird arrived there, Damayanti was reposing

'Damayanti and Her Divine Suitors', from *Tales of the Gods of India* by Shovana Devi. London, 1920.

in her park surrounded by her beauteous maids of honour. 'What a lovely bird!' cried Damayanti, with wonder-dilated eyes. 'Behold its graceful form, its wings all edged with gold!' Then she called out to the swan, saying: 'O wondrous bird, whence dost thou come, and hast thou any message for me?' The swan came close to her and suffered himself to be made captive by her perfect hand.

'O Princess!' he said, 'treat me not harshly. I come to thee as a messenger of love from Nala, King of Nishada. He is himself as beauteous as the God of Love and has no peer on Earth. The union of such a youth and maiden would be an union of the peerless with the peerless. Wed him, and thou shalt be the happiest of brides.'

Much did the maiden wonder at the bird's strange story and when he had delivered his message to her she set him free, saying: 'O sweet bird! speak in like manner unto Nala for me.'

'So be it,' said the swan, and flew back to Nala with her answering message of love.

Ere long a svayamvara was held for Damayanti, and many were the princes who came to woo her, allured by the stories of her beauty. The gods of Sumeru, equally enamoured of her rosy charms, came down to Earth to woo her. Most prominent among them were the four great guardians of the world: Indra, God of Heaven; Agni, God of Fire; Varuna, God of Waters; and Yama, God of Death.

Damayanti now stepped into the svayamvara hall, bejewelled from head to foot, bearing a garland of flowers to put round the neck of the one she would choose for her husband, and every eye and heart was entranced by her dazzling beauty. She was taken round to each of the assembled princes, according to the rite, until she came to where her lover, Nala, was seated; but great was her dismay when she beheld five Nalas, each indistinguishable from the other except by the eyes of gods.

Damayanti paused for a moment, garland in hand, and

then threw round the neck of her beloved, the real Nala, the wreath of bright flowers she carried in her hand. She had noticed that the gods, who had assumed his shape to baffle her, cast no shadows because they were spirits, and that their eyes never winked because they were the ever-wakeful guardian gods, and that their garlands were not withered, being woven of the unfading blooms of the groves of Paradise. By these tokens did the princess recognise the gods who had assumed the likeness of her lover in the hope of cheating her into choosing one of them. Turning to them, she said: 'Forgive me, O mighty gods, that I have not chosen my husband from among you. Since I heard the sweet endearing words of the golden-winged swan, Nala's messenger of love to me, I have pledged my heart to this prince, and the vow so pledged is sacred. Forgive me, therefore, ye guardians of the rulers of Heaven.'

Thus did Damayanti, the peerless, choose Nala for her lord with the gods themselves, her divine wooers, as witnesses. The happy pair then did homage before the gods, and these resplendent guardians of the Earth bestowed upon them divine nuptial gifts in reward for her constancy, and thereafter were borne back to Sumeru.

Love Conquers All

Ruskin Bond

❦

Long long ago there was a king who ruled over a large part of India. He was a great horseman, and when he rode he was like a strong wind rushing by. Horses knew and loved him, and because of his power over them he was known as Lord-of-Horses.

In spite of his fame and popularity, the king was unhappy, for no children had been born to him, and in India this was always considered a great calamity. He went from temple to temple, praying and offering sacrifices, but to no avail—it seemed as though the gods were displeased with him.

Finally he consulted the great sage Narada.

'How can I please the gods?' he asked. 'I have been married five years, but still there is no heir to the throne.'

'Build a new temple,' said Narada. 'Build a temple to Brahma the Creator.'

'I shall build the most beautiful temple in the land,' said the king, and he immediately summoned his best workmen and told them to build a temple taller than any other.

Ruskin Bond retells his favourite story from the *Mahabharata*.

'Let it be taller than three palm trees,' he said. 'Paint it gold within and gold without. A hundred steps of pure white marble must lead up to it.'

Within a few months a beautiful golden temple was built, surrounded by flowering trees and shrubs. And every day the king visited the temple, making special offerings to Brahma, God of Creation, and his wife Savitri, that they might send him a son.

His queen and his nobles, and even the sage Narada, had almost given up hope, when one day, as the king laid his offerings before the shrine, he thought he saw a figure growing out of the flames that had sprung up from his sacrifice. And then he heard a voice—the voice, he thought, of a goddess, because though it was small and sweet it filled the temple with its sound.

'You have pleased me with your devotion,' were the words he heard. 'I am Savitri, wife of Brahma. What is it you seek?'

His voice trembling, the king said, 'Goddess, I desire a son, so that my name may not perish from the land.'

'I will give you a daughter,' replied the clear sweet voice.

The fire died down and the figure faded.

And not long afterwards there was great rejoicing in the king's palace. A daughter was born to the queen—a girl so radiantly beautiful that her parents were convinced that she was heaven-born, and sent out a proclamation saying that the child was to be called 'Savitri' after the wife of Brahma.

•

As Savitri grew up, her father began to think about her marriage, and he decided that she should choose a husband for herself from among the princes of the neighbouring states. He had no intention of imposing his will upon her.

'Daughter,' he said one day, 'do you wish to marry? You

may, if you wish, visit the palaces of our neighbouring kings and choose a husband for yourself from among the princes. I know that you are as wise as you are lovely, and that your choice will be pleasing to me.'

Savitri decided that she would seek her husband not among her wealthy and royal neighbours, but among the remote dwellings of the hermits in the forest. She had her chariot prepared for a long journey, and ordered her drivers to take the path that led into the wilderness.

After driving through the forest for several hours, the chariot-drivers told Savitri that a hermitage lay ahead. Savitri and her handmaidens got down from the chariot and approached a small temple, beside which stood a hut made of leaves and branches.

Inside the hut they found an old man who, though blind and white-haired, had an upright bearing. He was, in fact, not a priest, but a king: many years ago he had gone blind and had been driven from his kingdom by a rival who took over his throne and threatened death to any of the king's family who tried to return.

As Savitri stood watching the blind old man, a youth on a black horse came riding through the forest and up to the door of the hut.

'He dresses like a peasant,' said Savitri to herself, 'but he sits on his horse like a prince.' And when she saw his face, her own lit up, for she knew that she had seen the man she would marry.

The youth dismounted, tethered his horse, greeted the old man with tender affection, and went into the hut.

'We need search no further,' said Savitri to her handmaidens. 'Let us ask the hospitality of these good people, and then in a few days we will return home.'

The old king made them welcome. He told them of his misfortunes and of how he, and his wife, and their little son Satyavan, had been driven from the kingdom of Shalwa twenty years ago, and had lived ever since among the hermits of the forest. Satyavan stood aside, watching Savitri, and falling further in love with her every moment. Not many days had passed before they had vowed to marry each other, but Savitri said that first she must return to her father's kingdom and obtain his consent to the marriage, after which she would come back to the forest and follow Satyavan for the rest of her life.

'But do not tell your parents as yet,' she said. 'Let me first speak to my father.'

Savitri returned to her father's palace and found him holding counsel with Narada. The sage had suggested that it was time a husband was found for Savitri.

'Well, here she is,' said the king, as Savitri approached. 'She will tell you whether or not she has found a husband.'

'Yes, father, I have,' she said, as she knelt at his feet for blessing. 'In his dress and his possessions he is a poor man's son, but by birth he is a prince.'

'And his name?'

'Satyavan.'

Before she could say another word, Narada, looking horrified, stood up and with raised hand, said: 'No, Princess, not Satyavan!'

'There can be no other,' said Savitri with a smile.

The king turned to Narada and asked: 'Is there something wrong with the youth? Is he not all that my daughter takes him for?'

'He is all that she says—'

'Then is he already betrothed? Is there a curse upon him?'

Narada bowed his head and in a low voice said: 'He is destined for an early death. Yama, the God of Death, has set his noose for him. Within a year the prince must die.'

Savitri went pale and almost fainted. But she summoned up all her courage and said, 'Narada, you have prophesied his doom, I can but pray and hope. But even the knowledge of this terrible fate cannot shake my purpose.

Satyavan shall be my husband for a year, even if for fifty I must be a widow!'

The sage stood silent, his head sunk upon his breast. Then finally he raised his hands towards Savitri in blessing.

'Peace be with you, daughter of the Lord-of-Horses,' he said, and turned and walked away.

ॐ

The next day it was announced that the princess Savitri would soon marry a prince in a distant region, and that, since the journey would be long and tedious, only her father would accompany her. Preparations were soon made, and the Lord-of-Horses and his beautiful daughter set out for the forest, They took with them many costly gifts for the parents of the bridegroom. But when the old king of the Shalwas heard what had brought them to his home, he was taken aback.

'But how can this be?' he asked. 'How will your heaven-sent daughter fare in this rough country? There are no maids to tend on her. And what shall we feed her? We eat the fruits of the forest. We sleep on an earthen floor.'

Savitri took the blind old man by the hand, and spoke to him so sweetly and gently that she removed all his fears.

That same evening, when Satyavan returned from hunting, Savitri was given to him in marriage. The only guests were the hermits who lived near by. All they brought as gifts were their blessings; and Savitri pleased them by removing her jewels and replacing her rich garments with humble clothes.

The Lord-of-Horses bade his daughter farewell, and rode alone back to his kingdom.

The days and weeks and months slipped by and it seemed to Satyavan that his wife grew lovelier and more gentle by the hour. No man was as happy as he. Savitri, too, was happy; but as the day of doom approached, she became quiet and pensive. She decided she would not leave his side by day or night. So she watched and waited, and seldom slept.

One morning the blind old king asked Satyavan to go to a part of the forest where there was a bamboo grove. He asked him to cut and bring home several stout pieces of bamboo.

When Satyavan set out, Savitri decided to follow not far behind. 'I will watch the dancing peacocks,' she told him.

Satyavan, whistling cheerfully, soon reached the place where the bamboos grew, and raised his axe. He had scarcely lifted it above his head for the first stroke, when it fell from his hands. He gave a cry of pain and sank to the ground.

Savitri, following close behind, knew that the fatal moment was at hand. She ran forward and took his head in her arms. A shadow fell over them, and she became aware of a terrible form bending over her. It was tall and gaunt, greenish in hue, and with eyes of a fiery red. He carried a noose in one of his hands.

This was Yama, the God of Death.

Savitri rose slowly from the ground, and bending low before Yama, said: 'What do you want, O mighty one?'

'I have come for Satyavan, whose term of life is ended.' And Yama leant forward and drew the prince's soul right out of his body.

Then, turning to the south, he fled at lightning speed, in the direction of his kingdom, Patola.

But Savitri, too, was fleet of foot. Love lent her wings, and she followed close at Yama's heels. They came at last to the edge of the world, beyond which no mortal may pass alive, and here the God of Death stopped and spoke.

'Return, Savitri! You have followed far enough. Return and bury your husband's body with due rites.'

'No, great Yama,' answered Savitri. 'When I wed my

lord, I vowed to follow him, wherever he went or was taken. I have done no wrong since I made that vow, and so the Gods have no power over me to make me break it.'

'That is true,' said Yama, 'and your answer pleases me. Ask a boon of me—but not the gift of your husband's life!'

Savitri thought for a moment, and then asked that the old king of the Shalwas should regain his sight.

'It is granted,' said Yama. 'Now return. No mortal may pass this spot alive.'

But Savitri stood her ground. She knew that no one loved Yama, that he was friendless even among the gods, so she decided to flatter him.

'Is it true, O Yama, that a mortal is pleasing to the gods if she mingles with those who are virtuous?'

'It is true,' said Yama.

'Then you cannot force me to go, for you are virtuous, and I become more pleasing to the gods every moment I stay beside you.'

Yama was delighted and told Savitri that, for her good sense, she might obtain another boon from him.

'Then grant that my father-in-law may regain his former kingdom,' she said. Yama assented and told her for the third time to go back and find her husband's body before it was devoured by jackals.

'It does not matter,' said Savitri, 'if the jackals devour the corpse. Of what use is the body without the soul? Another body can be found for the soul, if it is released from your noose, but never another soul for the body.'

'You speak with more wisdom than most mortals,' said the God. 'Yet one more boon will I grant you.'

'Grant me a hundred sons, O mighty Yama,' cried Savitri. And when the God bowed his head in assent, she laughed and clapped her hands. 'If you are indeed a God who keeps his word with men, then release the soul of Satyavan. There is no other man that I can marry, and only by bringing him back to life can you grant me the sons you have promised!'

Yama realized that Savitri had been allowed, by a greater power than he, to triumph over him; so he loosened the coil of his rope, and Satyavan's soul flew up into the air and back to the forest where his body lay. Some time later, Savitri reached the same place and found her husband lying just as she had left him. She lifted his head, and he opened his eyes and stretched himself and yawned.

'I must have fallen asleep,' he said. 'Why did you not wake me before? It is almost sunset.'

Hand in hand they walked home, and on the way she told him all that had happened. And when they came home they found their father and mother rejoicing with the other hermits because the old man had regained his sight, and his enemy had been slain and the people wished their former ruler to return to them.

The next day Savitri and Satyavan, with their parents, returned to Shalwa, and there they all lived happily for the rest of their lives. We are told that Savitri and Satyavan lived together for four hundred years, and that they had a hundred sons, as Yama had promised.

Today, when anyone wishes to pay a wife the highest compliment, it is said that she is like Savitri, who brought back her husband's soul from the edge of the world.

Gwashbrari and Westarwan

Flora Annie Steel

Ages ago, when the world was young and the mountains[*] had just reared their heads to the heavens, Westarwan was the highest peak in all Kashmir. Far away in the west Nanga Parbat stood where it stands now, but its snowy cap only reached to Westarwan's shoulder, while Haramukh looked but a dwarf beside the giant king. But if Westarwan was the tallest, Gwashbrari was the most beautiful of mountains. Away in the northeast she glinted and glittered with her sea-green emerald glaciers, and Westarwan gazed and gazed at her loveliness till he fell in love with the beautiful Gwashbrari; but her heart was full of envy, and she thought of nothing but how she might humble the pride of the mighty king that reared his head so high above the rest of the world. At last the fire of love grew so hot in Westarwan's heart that he put aside his pride and called

---

'Gwashbrari and Westarwan', from 'Folklore from Kashmir' by F. A. Steel with notes by Lt. R. C. Temple. *The Indian Antiquary* Vol. XI, 1882.

[*] All the mountains mentioned in this tale are prominent peaks in Kashmir and belong to the mid-Himalayan range. The Westarwan ridge is the longest spur into the Valley of Kashmir. This and the remarkably clear tilt of the strata doubtless suggested this fanciful and poetical legend.

aloud to Gwashbrari, 'O beautiful far-away mountain, kiss me, or I die.'

But Gwashbrari answered craftily, 'How can I kiss you, O Proud King, when you hold your head so high? Even if I could stand beside you my lips would not reach your lips, and behold how many miles of hill and dale lie between us.'

But still Westarwan pleaded for a kiss, till Gwashbrari smiled, and said, 'Those above must stoop, Sir King. If you would have a kiss forget your pride, reach that long length of yours towards me, and I will bend to kiss you.'

Then Westarwan, stretching one great limb over the vale of Kashmir, reached over hill and dale to Gwashbrari's feet, but the glacier-hearted queen held her flashing head higher than ever, and laughed, saying: 'Love humbles all.'

And this is why Westarwan lies for ever stretched out over hill and dale, till he rests his head on Gwashbrari's feet.

The Story of Khamba and Thoibi

G. H. Damant

In the village of Moirang in the country of Manipur, there lived Purelba, slayer of five tigers, son of Pachelba—a prince who had fled from his native village where he had quarrelled with his brother the king.

Songlel Lalthaba, the king of Moirang, had two grandsons; the eldest was Jarathong Yamba—who afterwards became king—and the second, Chingkhutol Haiba—who became the jubraja, the crown prince.

King Jarathong Yamba, deeming that Purelba had become famous by having killed the five tigers, gave him his own wife, Gnangko Reima Yareltom Pokpi, and he married her and begot a daughter called Khamnu and a son Khamba. To show his great liking for Purelba, the king also gave him the lands of Nongtholba, Lonoirakpa and Khada Halba, and also the salt well at Tarbung and the Naga villages of Laisang and Kharam Lairel; he also received a tribute of pepper from the Nagas. Purelba had formed a friendship with Thonglel, Chouba, and Kabui Salang Maiba Kharingnag Chumba. When Khamba was born his three friends told him that it would be well to go to the king

'The Story of Khamba and Thoibi', a Manipuri folk tale translated by G. H. Damant, *The Indian Antiquary*, Vol. VI. 1877.

and ask him to give the child a name. The king told them to wait a while, and after some consideration came back and said, 'As I have made you wait, let us call your son Khamba.'* The father was pleased with it, and gave a *chei*, i.e. two *tolas*, of gold.

Now the king Jarathong Yamba and the jubraja Chingkhutol Haiba had no children, although the king had fifteen wives and the jubraja eleven, so they went and worshipped the god Thangjing, but still the king had no child. However, Khurambi, the first wife of the jubraja, bore a daughter. The king was very much pleased, and said, 'As I have no child, this daughter of my brother's will be celebrated above all others; let us therefore call her Thoibi (i.e. 'famous').'

One day after this, as Purelba was returning from the palace he fell ill, and called his two friends Thonglel and Chouba, and said to them, 'My friends, I am very ill and about to die, therefore I wish to speak to you. My friend Chouba, you have a son, Phairoichamba, and I have a daughter, Khamnu; make her your daughter and marry her to your son.' So saying he called the child who was then five years old and gave her away. Then he said to Thonglel, 'You, my friend, although you have nine wives, have no child; therefore take my children Khamnu and Khamba for your own, and also take all my clothes, turban, *dao*, spear, hunting dress, war dress, necklaces and ornaments, and if you hear of any one ill-treating my children protect them like a father; and you, my friend Chouba, protect their land and wood, as would a mother, and guard them should any one make them slaves or seize their cattle; and you, Thonglel, be a father to them.' With these words Purelba died.

After this Khamba gradually began to sit up and to walk, and when Khamnu was old enough to nurse her little

* The Manipuri word *khamba* means 'to restrain, to make to stop'.

brother her mother died. The two friends, Thonglel and Chouba, came and burnt her body, and Thonglel said to Khamnu and Khamba, 'My children, come to my house and I will be your father; you have none else left to care for you.' But Khamnu refused to leave her father's house, although Thonglel told her that her father on his deathbed had entrusted all his property to him; and, as it would be spoiled if it remained there, he took it all away with him. When he reached home he said to his wife, Thungselbi, 'In case I die or fall ill, or forget it, remember that this property all belongs to my friend Purelba and his wife.' But afterwards, through the miraculous power of a god, he forgot all about it, and so did the children. In the meantime Khamnu supported her little brother by begging.

One day, as it fell out, Khamnu went to beg at the house of Ningollakpa of Moirang, and it happened that Thoibi had come there to play at *kang*,[*] and was eating with the other ladies of the royal family. When Khamnu came up, the servant at the door would not let her enter, saying that the ladies were at dinner; but just at that moment Thoibi came out to bathe, and seeing Khamnu asked who she was. Khamnu replied that she had come to beg, and that her name was Khamnu and she was the daughter of a Kumal.^{**} Thoibi felt pity for her, and asked her where she lived, and why she came to beg, and whether she had no father or mother or brother. Khamnu said she had no father or mother, but supported one young brother, and lived in the quarter of Chingali. Thoibi pitying her replied, 'Let us be friends and eat together.' So saying she took her among the

---

* This is a game like skittles, but on a small scale. The *kang* is the seed of a large king of creeper called *gila* in Bengal; it is propelled by the finger at a number of pins set in a row. It is principally played by the Manipuri women.

** The Manipuris are said to be derived from four tribes—Moirang, Luang, Kumal and Meithei; they have now all assumed the name Meithei, which tribe seems to have conquered the rest.

other royal ladies and made her eat, and gave her
well-cooked rice and vegetables for her brother, and told
her to take home with her as much of the rice, fish, and salt
that was left as she could carry. Thoibi then asked her
brother's name, and Khamnu told her it was Khamba. Then
Thoibi said, 'Sister, all the royal ladies are going tomorrow
to fish in the Logtak (a lake in the south of Manipur); come
with me and steer my boat; but it is not proper that you
should come among so many people with such ragged
clothes; stay awhile.' And she sent her servant Senu into
the house and brought a dhoti, chadar, and pagri for
Khamba and a *phanek* and chadar for Khamnu,[*] and gave
her some *sel*[**] as well.

Khamnu returned home and gave the rice and clothes
to her brother. Khamba, finding the food very good, asked
her where she had got it. Thereupon she told him how she
had formed a friendship with Thoibi, who had given her the
food and clothes, and invited her to steer her boat next day
when she went fishing; and she told Khamba to stay at
home and guard the house. Early next morning the ladies
of the royal family, with Thoibi and Khamnu, went down
to Logtak, and cast their nets and caught many fish.

Towards evening Khamba, thinking that he might
meet Thoibi, determined to go to the lake. So he took a boat
and fortunately came to the very place where his sister and
Thoibi were. Directly he and Thoibi met they fell in love
with each other, and Thoibi asked Khamnu if she knew who
he was. The girl replied that he was her own brother, and
turning to him asked him why he had come. He said she
had been a long time returning, so he had come to meet her.
His sister said she would follow, and he returned home.

---

[*] The dress of a Manipuri woman consists of a skirt called *phanek*, worn
straight across the breast under the armpits, a jacket called *phurit*,
and a *chadar*; the two latter are often dispensed with.

[**] A small brown coin used in Manipuri; about 45 to the rupee.

Thoibi, Khamnu and the rest followed, and Thoibi gave Khamnu a great quantity of fish for herself and her brother to eat.

Now Thoibi had been very much pleased with Khamba, and could not forget him, so she told Khamnu she would pay her a visit at her own house. Then she went away, and they all went, each to her own house. In the evening Thoibi took her servant Senu with her to carry some food, and went to Khamba's house. Khamnu saw her coming and saluted her, and Thoibi asked her how she and her brother managed to live. She replied that through their poverty they were forced to live by begging. Thoibi replied, 'Your house does not look like the house of poor people, but seems to belong to a great officer: tell me the truth.' Khamnu said, 'My father was an officer under the king of Kumal—so I have heard my father and mother say.' Thoibi was secretly rejoiced to hear that, and said, 'It is very late, we cannot go alone; tell your brother to see us home.' So Khamba went with them and on the way he and Thoibi agreed that they would be betrothed, and took an oath to be faithful to each other, and Khamba came back after seeing Thoibi to her home.

Some time after this the two divisions of the village of Moirang played a match at hockey.[*] Kongyamba was the captain of the lower division, and Khamba of the upper division. Previous to this, Khamba had not been renowned among the people, but God made him victorious at hockey, and when he defeated Kongyamba, all the people of the upper division were glad; and after this his father's friend Chouba introduced him to all as the son of Purelba.

A short time afterwards all the people assembled and

---

[*] Hockey was the great national game of the Manipuris, whether on foot or horseback; it was played by all classes, from the Raja downwards. To be a good hockey-player was a sure way of rising to notice in the state.

obtained leave from the king to hold a festival[*] in honour
of the God Thangjing. Kongyamba was appointed to collect
flowers to decorate the lower division of the village, and
Khamba to do the same for the upper division, and Chouba
then introduced him to the king. Early next morning
Kongyamba and Khamba went to pick flowers, as the
festival was to be held on the following day. Kongyamba
told Khamba to go up the mountain, while he would remain
where he was; and Kongyamba picked *haukeroi*[**] flowers
but Khamba climbed a tree and gathered *mellai*[***] flowers,
and when they had gathered sufficient they both returned
home. Later, Thonglel, his father's friend, called Khamba
and gave him all his father's clothes and ornaments, and
taught him to dance. When the king and all the people were
assembled for the festival, Kongyamba presented flowers
to the deity and the king, and distributed the rest among
the people, and Khamba did the same; and the king, seeing
that the flowers which Khamba had brought were out of
season, gave him a reward. After that the boys and girls
began to dance, and the king made Khamba and Thoibi
dance together, and all the people talked of their beauty.
When the festival was at an end, the king and others made
obeisance to the deity, which was taken away, and then
they all returned home.

After some time it happened that wrestling and
running matches were held, and Kongyamba was chosen
captain of the lower village, and Khamba of the upper

---

[*]   This festival is called Laiharouba, and is still commonly held; it is a
      remnant of paganism which has not succumbed to the Hinduism now
      prevailing in the country. The god in whose honour the festival is held
      is placed in the midst, and all the men and women, both married and
      unmarried, dance round it gaily decked with flowers, songs are sung,
      and the village fiddlers attend.

[**] A kind of red coxcomb.

[***] A kind of yellow and brown orchid; it flowers in October. It is one of the
      most handsome of the orchid tribe.

village. There were fifteen competitors on either side, and the starting point was at Kwakta. Khamba won the race, whereupon Khamba and Kongyamba wrestled together, and Khamba was victorious. He was also successful in jumping, tossing the *caber*, and putting the stone; and the king, declaring him the best man, made him a present of clothes.

Some days after this the time came for the *maibi** to sit at the shrine of the god in order to consult the oracle. Now Kongyamba determined that Khamba must die, so disguising himself as the *maibi* he sat before the god, and told the king,—'The god declares in a dream that if you can catch the bull which feeds at Ikop and offer it to him, your life will be long and your people happy.' So the king assembled all his officers and people and said, 'If the bull which feeds at Ikop can be caught and offered to the god, my life will be long. Is there any among you who can catch it?' As no one answered, Khamba came forward and saluted the king, and said he would undertake the task. The king was delighted to hear it, and said, 'If you succeed, I will give you my niece Thoibi in marriage; but the bull grazes on the lands of the king of Kumal; we must send word to him.' Thus an officer named Thangarakpa was sent, who told the king of Kumal about the oracle and he agreed to let them catch the bull, proposing that his friend the king of Moirang and he should go together to see the sight.

When Thangarakpa returned, the king ordered a proclamation to be made, and the next day the king of Moirang and his people, all assembled to see the sight, the two kings sitting side by side on the platform. Khamba

---

* The *maibis* are a kind of priests, or rather priestesses: for they are generally, though not always, women. They preside at the different festivals, act as fortune-tellers, and are reputed to have some skill in medicine.

came forward and saluted them, saying he was ready, and he and the bull engaged in a deathly struggle. At last he threw the bull down, and bound him with a rope and brought him before the two kings. The king of Moirang was much pleased, and gave him a present of clothes, and a gold necklace and bracelets. The king of Kumal asked whose son he was, and the other king replied, 'He is of your family, for he is the son of Purelba.' The king of Kumal said, 'Then he is my cousin, for Purelba was my father's elder brother. Treat him kindly.' The other king said, 'I have given him my niece Thoibi in marriage.' And the king of Kumal replied, 'Then you and I have become relations. Let us go now.' So they both of them went away home, and the bull was offered to the god of Moirang.

In the course of time it was determined to hold a shooting match, and every one put on his best clothes. Kongyamba was ordered to pick up the arrows shot by the king, and Khamba those of the jubraja. Now Thoibi had made a very handsome jacket, and when she heard that Khamba was to collect the arrows shot by her father she called her servant Senu and told her to give it to Khamba, and tell him to wear it the next day at the festival. After she had done so, her father the jubraja asked her where the jacket was, as he wished to wear it, but she said she had sold it and could not give it to him.

So the king and the people of Moirang went to the place where the archery match was held. The king shot first, and Kongyamba picked up his arrow and gave it back to him. Then the jubraja shot, and Khamba picked up his arrow, but as he was giving it back, the jubraja saw that he was wearing his daughter's jacket, and grew angry, declaring that he would not give his daughter to him, but to Kongyamba. So he called Kongyamba and said to him, 'I will give you my daughter Thoibi, and you may bring the fruit[*] for the marriage in seventeen days to me.' When Khamba's father's friends Thonglel and Chouba heard this, they came with Khamba and saluted the jubraja and pleaded with him, 'Do not dismiss Khamba in your anger.' But the jubraja answered, 'The daughter I have reared I have given away, there is nothing left.' The king was inwardly displeased to hear it, and retired to his palace, while the jubraja and all the people returned home.

The jubraja called Thoibi and told her that he had given her to Kongyamba; but she secretly determined that she would not consent, and went to her mother, the first queen, and said, 'My father has given me to Kongyamba, and told me to marry him, against my will.' The queen replied, 'The king gave you to Khamba for having caught the bull; tell him to come and marry you.' So she sent word to Khamba through her servant Senu. Early next morning Khamba took some fruit from his father's friend Kabui Senang Maiba, and carried it home with him. And the same morning Kongyamba brought his fruit for the marriage, but as Thoibi did not love him she pretended to be ill and he returned home. After this, on the queen's advice, Khamba brought his fruit, but Thoibi did not go with him, as the jubraja was angry and would not eat of the fruit that he had brought. So Thoibi put it aside carefully to give to her father when he was in a good humour. Meanwhile the jubraja went to hunt wild beasts at Tarbul, but was not successful, and as he was returning the god Thangjing inspired him with a great desire to eat some of Thoibi's fruit, so that when he reached home he asked her for some. She prepared the fruit which Khamba had brought, and gave it to him. He said, 'My daughter, this fruit is very good, where did you

---

[*] It is customary in Manipur for the bridegroom, before the marriage, to bring a present of fruit and vegetables to the bride's house, which is taken by her relations. It appears to be considered equivalent to a formal offer of marriage. It is called *Haejing puba*.

get it?' She replied, 'It is the fruit which Khamba brought, and which you refused to eat.' At that he grew very angry, and said, 'What! Have you given me the fruit which I refused to eat before?'

The jubraja thought in his heart that Khamba had bewitched his daughter, so he determined to have him beaten, and sent a servant to call Kongyamba secretly. Kongyamba came and saluted him, and the jubraja took him aside and said, 'Call Khamba to Khauri bazar and assemble your friends and relations to beat him, for he has bewitched my daughter, whom I gave to you.' Kongyamba went away rejoicing and assembled all his friends and relations, and called Khamba, and took them all to Khauri bazaar.

The jubraja secretly took one of the king's elephants called Gnangkharakpa Saranghalba, and went to the same place and said to Khamba, 'You have spoken softly to my daughter and made her mad; now if you will at once promise to give her up I will not beat you, but if you refuse, your grave shall be in this bazaar.' Khamba replied, 'Jubraja, even though you do not love me, yet when I caught the bull you and the king gave your daughter to me in the presence of all the people; and moreover she and I are betrothed, and have taken an oath to be faithful to each other, so I cannot give her up.' The jubraja hearing this became very angry, and said he would kill him. Khamba said, 'I will abide by the constancy of your daughter, and will never turn my face away from her.'

The jubraja then told Kongyamba to assemble his men to beat Khamba, and he and all his men rushed in and attacked Khamba. The latter girt up his clothes and attacked them in turn without turning his face away; but they were so many that they overcame him and beat him severely, and the dust rose in such clouds that their bodies could not be seen. There were thirty of them, so that he could not resist them. Then the jubraja became still more angry, and said, 'If he acts like this in my presence I will kill him at once; bring the elephant.' So all the men seized Khamba, and began to tie him to the elephant's foot.

Now, while this was going on, Thoibi was asleep, but the god came to her in a dream and told her that Khamba was being killed in the bazaar. She opened her eyes and wondered what it was, and then she called her servant Senu, and took a knife in her hand and went out. When the jubraja and the men who were tying Khamba to the elephant's foot saw her they all fled.

Thoibi went up to the elephant and said to him, 'Elephant, if you kill my lover, trample me under foot and kill me too,' and she took an oath to die under the elephant's feet. The elephant, seeing she was a good woman and had taken an oath, lowered his tusks to the ground and trumpeted; and she, seeing Khamba, asked the elephant to undo the rope by which he was tied, and as he did so, she said to Khamba, 'My dear, have you suffered all this for my sake?' and they both wept together.

Meanwhile Khamba's sister Khamnu, and his father's friends Thonglel and Chouba, hearing the news, ran up from all sides. When they saw Khamba, Thonglel and Chouba both grew very angry, and said, 'Bring Phairoichamba with you and come to the palace.' So they all went and found the jubraja sitting there. Thonglel said with anger, 'Who has beaten my son?' He had come there with many followers, wearing his sword, spear and shield, and all his war dress and ornaments; and the people, when they saw the numbers with him, and his angry looks, were all afraid. Thoibi told the king all that had happened, and the king was greatly displeased when he heard that Khamba had been beaten, and went to his throne-room to give his judgement in the matter. He decided that the jubraja was at fault, and forbade him to enter the palace again, and ordered all the men who had beaten Khamba to be themselves beaten. But when Kongyamba was about to

182   G. H. Damant

be beaten, Khamba saved him by saying that he was not at
fault—all the blame was with the jubraja. So Khamba and
all the people returned home, and the king ordered them to
take care that his servant Khamba did not die, putting him
in the charge of the royal doctor and instructing Thonglel
and Chouba to see that he had proper food while he was ill.

One day shortly after this her father the jubraja said
to Thoibi, 'For five days I have been trying to persuade you
to marry Kongyamba; why do you still persist in refusing
him?' Thoibi replied, 'Both you and my uncle the king
promised me to Khamba when he caught the bull, and I
have taken an oath to be his slave; I will not live with
Kongyamba.' At this answer the jubraja grew angry, and
said, 'If you do not obey me, your father, I will sell you as a
slave to my friend Tamurakpa at Kubbo, and I will take the
full price for you and spend it in feasting on fish.' Thoibi
answered, 'Whatever my father says is right.'

Early next morning the jubraja, saying he would make
a slave of Thoibi, called five of his servants and gave them
orders concerning her. And she, seeing that her father
intended to carry out his purpose, sent her servant Senu to
Khamba secretly to tell him about it—how her father had
made a slave of her, and that five men were appointed to
conduct her to Tamurakpa. So Khamba went and waited
quietly on the road, with a bamboo stick in his hand, and
when he saw Thoibi he said sadly, 'I have nothing else to
give you; take this and think of it as me.' So he gave her the
stick, and she went on her way, while he went sorrowfully
home.

When Thoibi sat down to rest by the roadside, she
broke the stick in two pieces on the spot and called God to
witness that if she were true and faithful the bamboo[*]
should sprout, and she planted one piece there and it

_____

[*] The clump of bamboos which grew from the stick, and the stone with
Thoibi's footprint, are still shown, as is Khamba's coat, which is kept
at Moirang, the scene of the story. It is said to be of gigantic size.

sprouted. After going a little further on the way she saw a large stone, and she said, 'If I am chaste and have truly chosen Khamba, may the stone become soft,' and she put her foot on it, and the footprint was left. When she arrived at the house of Tamurakpa, the five servants told her that she was not really sold, but that her father had sent her there to frighten her, and they asked Tamurakpa to treat her kindly, and went away. Tamurakpa called his daughter Changning Khombi, and told Thoibi to make friends with her and live there happily.

After three months' time the jubraja felt pity for his daughter, and called his five slaves and told them to fetch her back, and next morning he sent for Kongyamba and said to him, 'Today my daughter Thoibi will return from Tammu; wait for her on the road and try and persuade her to go to your house. If she refuses and escapes from you, say no more to me about her, for I will not give her again.' Kongyamba saluted gladly and went away, and his father and mother and all his relations waited in his house, expecting Thoibi to come. Meanwhile he mounted his horse and taking two servants with him, waited on the road for Thoibi to come. Now Senu, the servant of Thoibi's mother, heard the news and told Khamba secretly, and he told his sister Khamnu, but was undecided whether he should go to meet Thoibi or not. Meanwhile Tamurakpa told Thoibi that her father had sent for her, and she must go home, and he gave her some silk and other presents.

Now Thoibi, thinking Khamba would have heard the news, had made him a jacket and a full suit of clothes. Before she started she put on her ornaments and best clothes, and made obeisance to the household god of Tamurakpa, praying that she might be united with' her lover; then she saluted Tamurakpa and his wife, and he blessed her and told her that her wish would come to pass. And her friend Changning Khombi gave her a present, and hoped she might succeed in her wish. So she set out with her father's five slaves, and to her sorrow met Kongyamba on the road; for she did not love him; but he was very glad, and tried to persuade her to go with him by saying that her father had given her to him. Thoibi pretended to be glad outwardly, and sat down near him, but she put the stick which Khamba had given her between them, and thought of it as if it were Khamba himself, and determined to run away to him. At last she hit on a plan, and said she felt feverish. Kongyamba asked how she could be cured, and she said that if she could mount a horse and ride it till she perspired she would be well. So Kongyamba had his horse brought, and Thoibi put the saddle on her head, and saluted it, and saluted all the gods, praying that they would bring her to Khamba's house. Then she mounted the horse and galloped him up and down, but when she was at some little distance she galloped away, and by the help of the gods, who looked favourably upon her because she had saluted them, she arrived safely at Khamba's house. He and his sister Khamnu received her joyfully, and Kongyamba's horse was let loose.

Meanwhile Kongyamba, tracking the footprints of the horse, came to the front door and saw Thoibi in the verandah, and thinking that there would certainly be a quarrel he went away quietly, and told his father and mother how Khamba had taken Thoibi away and got the better of him. He said he would go next day to the king and demand justice. Meanwhile his family remained in the house.

Thoibi's servants brought all the things which Tamurakpa had given her to Khamba's house, and they all remained there that day, and word was sent to the jubraja that Thoibi was there.

Next day, early in the morning, all the officers of Moirang assembled before the king to decide the dispute between Khamba and Kongyamba; but while it was being heard, news came that a man had been killed by a tiger at

Khonentak. Then the king said to Khamba and Kongyamba, 'This news has come while we are hearing your dispute, so whichever of you can kill the tiger shall have my niece, and let God be the witness.' They both agreed, and all the people were witnesses thereto. So the people surrounded the tiger,[*] and built a fence round the place where he was, and early the next morning the king and all the people went to see the sight. As Khamba was starting, Thoibi said to him, 'If I am faithful and pure, you will certainly kill the tiger,' and she saluted her god and remained at home. Khamba and Kongyamba, each taking his weapons—spear and *dao*—and two servants, went to the place where the tiger was.

They knelt before the king, and he gave *paan* to each of them, and told them to be careful not to be killed, saying if one was wounded the other was to protect him. The two friends then saluted the king and all the people and went into the enclosure; the king and the people, holding their tiger-spears, waited to see the sight. As the two entered the tiger-net the people raised a shout. Khamba entered on the north side, and Kongyamba on the south. Kongyamba saw the tiger first and struck at it with his spear, but the tiger turned it aside with its paw and leaped up to seize him, and he, thinking the tiger would certainly bite him, caught it by the loins, and they both struggled together, but the tiger succeeded in biting Kongyamba on the back of the neck. Khamba then came up, and the tiger seeing him went away, and he took Kongyamba and gave him to his father to be taken care of. The king then ordered Khamba to go in again, and he went to the place where the tiger was, but when it saw him it ran away, and he chased it to strike it with his

---

[*] Tigers were caught in Manipur by surrounding the jungle in which they were with a net, outside of which a bamboo palisade was built, the whole place being closely surrounded by men armed with long, heavy spears; the tigers were generally shot, but in former days it was customary to spear them.

spear. The tiger ran round and round the enclosure, and
the people shouted at the sight. Now, since Thoibi was
faithful, through the might of the god to whom she had
prayed, the tiger was afraid of Khamba, and could not turn
its head towards him. In its efforts to escape it caught hold
of the platform where the king and a great number of people
were assembled. Khamba came up and put his foot on the
beast's tail, and when it turned to bite him he struck it in
the open mouth with his spear and killed it. The people were
all rejoiced, and presented the tiger to the king. Khamba's
father's friends Thonglel and Chouba came to the spot, and
the king was much pleased, and gave Thoibi to Khamba,
conferring upon him all the offices which his father held,
together with a handsome present, and he and all his people
went home. Kongyamba was taken to his home, where he
died. The jubraja was very glad, and Thoibi rejoiced when
she heard the news, and Khamba went home a great man.
Thoibi told Khamba he must be very tired, and gave him
rice and vegetables of all sorts to eat, which she had cooked
carefully, and as she was much pleased she attended on
him with great devotion.

Early the next morning the jubraja took Thoibi home,
and the king in his delight had a fine house built for
Khamba, and looked for a lucky day for the marriage,
preparing everything that was required—slaves, horses
and cattle. On the appointed day the king and all the
principal officers of Moirang went to the house of jubraja to
be present at the wedding, and Khamba with his father's
friends Thonglel and Chouba, and his brother-in-law
Phairoichamba, all of them wearing their ornaments, gold
bracelets and necklaces, came there too. And Thoibi came
wearing a red *hanek* embroidered with flowers, and her
dancing dress which was covered with bosses of gold and
silver, jewels, and glass, so that it shone brightly; she wore
golden bracelets and a golden necklace and her chain of gold
and coral fell down to her waist. The necklace on her bosom

lighted up the place; around her breast was fastened a beautiful jacket, and she wore a transparent scarf all bright with bosses of gold. Her appearance was like running water, and the hair on her head was like fresh flowers. When Thoibi came forth to her wedding, her arms were like lotuses, her legs were as beautiful as the inside of the stalk of a plantain tree and were like an elephant's tusks, her feet were arched as if she wore clogs, her colour was like turmeric, and her complexion like a *champaka* flower; she came forth like the full moon. All the people who had come to the marriage, when they saw Thoibi and Khamba, said they were beautiful like children of the gods, and never tired of looking at them. When the marriage was over, the king and the jubraja conducted them to their own house, with all the presents they had collected, and they saluted the king and the jubraja, who blessed them and returned to the palace.

After this Khamba gave his sister Khamnu in marriage to Phairoichamba, and conducted her to her husband's house, and gave her many slaves; and Thoibi gave her servant Senu in marriage, and gave her many slaves; and Thoibi and Khamba lived happily together in Moirang.

The Artist's Stratagem, or The Princess Who Was Resolved Never to Marry

Putlibai D. H. Wadia

Once upon a time there lived a great Raja, who had an only daughter. She was very beautiful and highly accomplished, and numbered amongst her other favourite pursuits that of hunting. She frequently went long distances on hunting excursions with a number of attendants, and penetrated the deepest recesses of the forest in search of sport.

One day, as she was galloping after a fine buck, she all of a sudden found herself in a dense forest, and saw that she had ridden considerably ahead of her followers. So she waited for a time and then climbed up a tree to try if she should see some signs of them in the far distance or find some way out of the forest; but on gaining the topmost branch she was appalled to see a great fire in the distance, evidently a part of the forest in flames.

The poor princess was, as it were, nailed to the spot at this awe inspiring sight, and stood there watching for hours the fork-tongued monster wrapping trees and shrubs, as well as the haunts and homes of numberless birds and

'The Artist's Stratagem', from 'Folklore in Western India' by Putlibai D. H. Wadia. *The Indian Antiquary,* Vol. XVII.

beasts in his fiery embrace, and destroying everything that came in its way. She could see whole herds of deer and cattle running about in a mad frenzy at their inability to find their way out of what seemed to them to be certain death, and birds of strange and varied plumage, suffocated by the thick smoke and unable to fly in the heavy atmosphere, charged with flying embers from the great fires around, uttering piercing screams of anguish before yielding to their inevitable doom.

In the midst of all this scene of woe the good princess was deeply moved to see a pair of wild geese straining every nerve to save their young ones from the clutches of the fire. Their difficulty was enhanced by the facts that the poor little creatures had as yet no wings, and were therefore totally unable to take care of themselves, and that it was beyond the old birds' strength to carry them in their beaks, as they tried hard to do, away from the closely pressing flames. So they flew about distractedly here and there, not knowing what to do, till the fire came too near to leave them any hopes of saving either themselves or their young ones. Just, however, as the flames were about to catch the nest, the old male bird, not wishing to sacrifice his own life, since he was unable to save those of his family, made a last desperate attempt, and with one effort found himself safe out of the reach of danger; while at the self-same moment the poor mother goose, as if resenting his selfish conduct, threw herself like a canopy over her unfortunate brood, and, with a wild scream of anguish, suffered herself to be burnt in the flames that just then closed over her and her innocent offspring.

The princess, who had watched all this with growing interest, was deeply touched at the sight. 'Ah,' said she to herself, 'how selfish and false these males are! I am sure they are the same all the world over, whether they be birds, beasts or men! I shall therefore neither have anything to do with them, nor trust them; nay, I shall continue single all my life rather than marry one of them.'

Hardly had the princess formed this rather rash resolve when she perceived her attendants coming towards her. They had come there to look for her, and when she got down and joined them they were highly delighted, for they had given her up for lost.

But from this day forth our heroine wore a grave look, shunned the society of all her male friends, and declared to her parents her firm determination never to enter the bonds of matrimony. This caused the old people great grief, and they implored her to tell them what had made her form so unwise a resolve. But the princess remained silent and would give them no explanation, so at last everybody came to believe that the king's daughter was not for marriage, and the number of suitors for her hand consequently fell off.

One day it happened that a great and renowned artist paid a visit to the great Raja's court, and by His Majesty's command executed some very rare paintings for the royal palace, and when the time came for his departure he begged of the beautiful Princess to give him a few sittings, to which she agreed after great hesitation, and allowed him to draw upon canvas a faithful likeness of her fairy face and figure. In a few days the picture was finished, but the artist, instead of handing it over to the princess, quietly went out of the city with it.

Now, the artist knew of an old Raja, who was a great connoisseur of paintings, so he went straight up to him with the Princess's portrait and sold it to him for a large sum of money. The picture was duly hung up in the great hall of audience, where it soon became the cynosure of all eyes and the topic of universal admiration, and all who looked upon it were struck with the enchanting beauty of the fair subject, and wondered very much who the original could be.

A few days after this it happened that the king's only son and the heir to his throne, who was away hunting when the picture was purchased, returned to the capital, and as he saw the picture fell head over heels in love with the lovely image on the canvas, without even taking the trouble of inquiring who the original was. He gave up all enjoyment, shunned all pleasure, and moped away in silence in a corner of the palace, to the great grief of his aged father, who, when he learned the cause of his son's sorrow felt very anxious about his health and sent messengers in search of the artist, with a view to finding out who was the subject of his picture. But all search proved fruitless, for the artist had long left the country and gone away, nobody knew where.

This vexed the young prince still more, and told so very badly upon his health and his temper that he grew highly capricious and headstrong, and regarded everyone with the greatest disfavour. One day the prime minister, an old and trusted servant of the State, happened to arouse him by mistake from a reverie into which he had fallen, and he lost his temper to such an extent as to sentence the poor old man to death there and then. Now, in the old Raja's palace the young prince's word being law, the old man saw nothing for it but to submit to his doom. As he was, however, being led away to execution the old Raja heard of it, and summoning his son into his presence, prevailed upon him to grant the old man a remission of his sentence for a few days, so that during that period he might make over charge of his public and private duties to other hands. To this the prince, after some difficulty, consented, and the old prime minister was allowed to go home to his family for the time.

He was resolved not to distress his family by telling them of the doom that awaited him, but they soon suspected from his pale and careworn look that something was wrong with him. They dared not question him, however, for some time, till his youngest daughter, who was a great favourite, at last put together all her courage, and, by her winning and persuasive ways, succeeded in learning from him the cause of his sorrow.

Now this young lady was very clever and full of resource, so she soon found a way of getting her father out of the difficulty. She went in person to the young prince, and, having succeeded in getting an audience, begged very hard of him to spare her old father's life till such time as she herself could go abroad and make an effort to find out who the original of that wonderful painting was, and in what part of the world she lived.

This pleased the prince very much, for in the scheme which the young lady unfolded to him he saw some prospect of realizing what was to him at the best a dream. He therefore readily withdrew his terrible mandate, and the good old prime minister was once more welcomed by the Raja, who gladly restored him to his former high position.

Soon after this the prime minister's daughter began to prepare for her journey. At first she set to work and drew a faithful copy of the great artist's picture, and then, dressing herself in male attire, set out on her travels as an artist bound to some distant country. She had an arduous task before her no doubt, for she hardly knew which way to go and where to inquire about the princess, but filial affection lent her courage, and she firmly resolved either to find out the princess or perish in the attempt.

So she travelled on and on for many months, and showed the picture wherever she halted, and to all she met, in the hope that it would be identified, but all to no purpose. At last, after more than a year's weary wandering, she arrived at a very distant and, to her, a very strange country, and there, to her great joy, everyone who saw the picture pronounced it to be a true and speaking likeness of the daughter of the Raja of the country: 'She,' they said, 'who is determined never to marry.'

'Never to marry!' said the fair artist in surprise. 'And what has made her form such a strange resolve?'

'Nobody can tell,' was the reply, 'even her parents do not know it.'

This news somewhat damped the ardour of the prime minister's daughter, for it was quite an unforeseen exigency and she was at a loss to know how her mission could be successful with one who was thus determined never to enter the bonds of matrimony.

Nevertheless, she took heart, and, hiring a house in close proximity to the Raja's palace, opened her studio there. Each day she sat there near a window which commanded a view of the palace, and worked away with her paints and brushes, till at last the Raja's attention was drawn towards her. So one day the Raja summoned her into his presence, and, after closely examining all her pictures and other works of art, extolled them highly and honoured her with a commission to execute some paintings for a palace which he was then building for the special use of his favourite and only daughter. The fair artist willingly obeyed the king's command, having in the meanwhile seen the princess several times with her own eyes, and made sure that she was no other than the original of the picture which had driven her prince well-nigh out of his senses. Accordingly, when the palace was ready, she went there and set to work painting the most artistic and lovely designs she could imagine on the walls, under the arches, and in every suitable place. The Raja and all the nobles and even the ladies of the court paid occasional visits to the palace, and they all, with one voice, admired both the workmanship of the artist and his choice of subjects. Each picture seemed to be a study in itself, and each had a history of its own which the artist related in a most interesting and winning manner. This latter fact drew a number of other female visitors to the palace, amongst whom were the ladies in immediate attendance on the princess, and these the artist thought were the persons most likely to know and tell her the reason why the princess shunned the society of men, and why she was determined never to enter into wedlock.

So she soon set to work and won them over to her with

her persuasive arts and delightful ways, and succeeded in learning from one of them, to whom the princess had confided her secret, the true story of her adventure in the forest and her consequent determination.

This was all the artist desired, and directly afterwards she drew on one of the walls of the drawing-room a picture just the reverse of what the princess had seen in the forest—a picture representing the infidelity of the female and the devotion of the male. For the geese she substituted a pair of antelopes, while in place of the princess she made to stand a very handsome young prince, so young, so brave, and so handsome, as to win the heart of any woman.

When this picture was ready our artist persuaded all the lady friends of the princess to request her to come and have a look at it, and at last one day, to her great joy, the princess honoured her with a visit, and going from picture to picture highly admired the artist's skill. When, however, she at last came to the picture of the antelopes and the prince she seemed greatly surprised and stood for a while lost in thought. Then, turning to the artist, she said:

'What is the history of this picture, my good friend?'

'O fair princess,' replied the disguised daughter of the prime minister, 'this picture represents an adventure the prince of our country had some time ago in a forest—perhaps it might not interest you much, madam, though it concerns us, loyal subjects of his father, very nearly, as this very episode in our prince's life has brought a change over his whole existence, for since that time he has shunned all thoughts of marriage, as he believes that the fair sex are all false and faithless and that it is of no use to trust them. This determination of his son and heir causes our good old Raja great grief, and has thrown a gloom over his whole court.'

'How strange!' cried the princess, interrupting the artist. 'Can males then be faithful and females false? I, for one, always believed it was the males who were false and faithless everywhere on earth; but now I see that there are two sides even to this question. I have as yet observed but one instance, and have since then been labouring under a false impression, but I shall not judge men so harshly hereafter.'

'Oh, I am so glad to hear you say so, good princess,' cried the artist in delight; 'how I wish our good prince too would see his mistake as you do yours.'

'Some one should point it out to him, I think,' said the princess, 'and perhaps, like me, he too might change his mind. As I have benefited by an episode in his life so he might profit by one in mine, and therefore you are at full liberty to relate my case to him and see what effect it has on him.'

'Surely I shall, with the greatest pleasure, when I get home,' replied the artist, her little heart fluttering with joy at this unexpected success in her undertaking.

Now, from this day it became known throughout the Raja's dominions that the fair princess had conquered her aversion to matrimony, and was once more open to offers of marriage, and there was again a crowd of eager aspirants to her hand. But the princess studiously discarded all their attentions, and seemed to derive no pleasure from their company. Her chief delight was in looking at the pictures the artist had painted in the new palace, and talking to her solely about the young prince, in whom she felt greatly interested.

The fair artist, thereupon, to secure the interests of her Raja's son, fanned the flame by telling the princess strange and vividly-coloured stories of his manliness, valour and virtues, till at last she inspired her with such a love for him that one day, being unable to contain herself, the princess expressed an earnest desire to see him. This was the very thing the clever young lady desired, and she readily promised to go back to her country and do all in her power to bring her prince to the feet of the fair princess by telling him her story and thereby creating in him a desire to see her.

Great was the joy both of the old prime minister, her father, and the gallant young prince when our fair artist returned home after a long absence, and related to them the successful termination of her mission. The old man hailed her as the saviour of his life, and the young prince loaded her with honours and precious gifts.

Immediately afterwards the prince set out with a grand cavalcade and a magnificent train of followers for the court of our fair heroine's father, and, needless to say, he was soon accepted as a worthy suitor for the fair princess's hand, and in the course of a few days their union was celebrated with due splendour and rejoicings.

Princess Pepperina

Flora Annie Steel

A bulbul and its mate lived in a forest and sang all day. At last the bulbul said, 'O husband, I should like some green chillies.' The obedient lover flew off at once to find some. He flew and he flew, and he flew: still not in one single garden could he find a single green chilli. There was no fruit at all on the bushes, or it was red. At last in a desolate place he came to a magnificent garden; tall mango trees shaded it, and innumerable flowers and fruits were to be seen, but not a single sign of life: no birds, no beasts, no insects. The bulbul flew down into the middle of the garden, and lo! there grew a single pepper plant, and on it hung one single large green chilli that shone like an emerald. So the bulbul flew home to his mate, and said, 'Come with me, dear wife, and I will show you the most beautiful green chilli you ever saw.'

Now the jinn to whom the garden belonged was asleep in a summer house; he generally slept for twelve years at a time, and then remained awake for twelve years. So he knew nothing about it when the bulbul and his wife arrived in the garden and began to eat his beautiful green chilli. It so happened, however, that the time for his awakening was

'Princess Pepperina', from 'Folklore in the Punjab' by F. A. Steel, with notes by R. C. Temple. *The Indian Antiquary*, Vol. X, 1881.

drawing near, so he grew restless and had bad dreams while the bulbul's wife was eating the chilli. At the end of that time she laid one green glittering egg on the ground beneath the pepper plant, and then she and her mate flew away.

Just then the jinn woke, and, as usual, went at once to see how his pet pepper plant was getting on. He found it pecked to pieces. Great was his sorrow and dismay; he wondered what had done the damage, knowing well that neither bird, beast nor insect lived in the garden. 'Some horrid creeping thing from the world outside must have stolen in while I was asleep,' said he to himself. 'I will search for it and kill it.' So he began to search and found nothing but the shining glittering green egg. He took it to the summer-house, wrapped it up in cotton wool, and laid it in a niche in the wall.

Every day he looked at it, and sighed to think of his lost chilli; but one morning when he went to the niche, lo and behold! the egg had disappeared, and in its place sat the loveliest little maiden. She was dressed from head to foot in emerald green, and round her throat hung a single large emerald, shaped just like a green chilli. The jinn, who was good-hearted and fond of children, was delighted, and made it the business of his life to tend the Princess Pepperina, for that she told him was her name.

Now when the Princess Pepperina was about twelve years old, it became time for the jinn to go to sleep again, and he racked his brains—what was to become of the princess meanwhile? It so happened that a king and his minister were hunting in the forest, and came upon the garden. Curious to see what was inside, they climbed over the wall, and found the beautiful Princess Pepperina seated by the pepper plant. The young king fell in love with her at once, saying, 'Come and be my bride.'

'Not so,' said the Princess modestly. 'The jinn who owns this garden is as my father, and you must ask him;

unfortunately he has a habit of eating men sometimes.' But when she looked at the young king her heart softened; she had never seen any one so handsome and beautiful; so she said, 'Hide yourselves in the garden, and when the jinn returns I will question him.'

No sooner had the jinn entered the summer-house than he called out, *'Ho, ho, ho, manushgandh! manushgandh!'**

Then the Princess said: 'Dear jinn, eat me if you will, for there is no man here, only me.' But the Jinn kissed her, and caressed her, saying, 'Dear life! I would sooner eat bricks and mortar.' After that the princess asked him what would happen to her when he fell asleep, and the good jinn became sad and troubled at the thought of her loneliness. At last he said: 'If I could only marry you to some young man, but there are none hereabouts: besides, your husband must be as beautiful as you are, and it will be a hard task to find such a one.' Then the Princess Pepperina was rejoiced, and said: 'Do you promise to marry me to any one, provided he is as beautiful as I am?'

The jinn promised faithfully; then the princess clapped her hands, and out of a thicket came the young king.

When he stood beside the princess holding her hand, even the jinn was obliged to confess that never was such a handsome couple seen. So the marriage was performed hurriedly, for already the jinn began to yawn; but when he said goodbye to the princess, he wept so that it kept him awake, and he followed them in his thoughts till he longed to see her face once more. Then he changed himself into a dove, and flew after her, and fluttered above her head. When he had had a gook look at her, and saw she was happy, he flew back again to his garden, and yawned, but the green mantle of Princess Pepperina floated before his eyes and kept him awake. So he changed himself into a

---

* 'I smell a man, I smell a man.' This is a common expression put into the mouth of jinn, etc. in stories, and is the counterpart apparently of the English 'Fee, fa, fo, fum, I smell the blood of an Englishman.'

hawk, and flew after her, circling round her head. When he had assured himself of her welfare, he flew back to his garden and tried to sleep. But the soft eyes of the Princess seemed to look into his, so that he could not close them. At last he changed himself into an eagle, and soared far up into the sky, till with his bright piercing eyes he saw the princess away on the horizon entering a king's palace. Then he was satisfied, yawned and went to sleep.

Now the young king continued passionately in love with his new wife, but the other women were jealous, especially after she gave birth to the most lovely young prince that ever was seen; so they thought and thought how they might kill her or lay a snare for her. Every night they came to the door of the Queen's room and whispered to see if she was awake, saying, 'The Princess Pepperina is awake, but all the world is fast asleep.' Now the emerald which the Princess wore round her neck, was a talisman, and always told the truth. So it answered at once, 'Not so! The Princess is asleep; it is the world that wakes.' Then the wicked women shrunk away, for they knew they had no power to harm the Princess so long as the talisman was round her neck.

At last, one day when the Princess was bathing she took off the talisman, and left it by mistake in the bathing place. That night when the wicked women came and whispered, 'The Princess Pepperina is awake, but all the world is fast asleep,' the truthful talisman called out from the bathing place: 'Not so! The Princess is asleep, it is the world that wakes.' Then knowing by the direction whence the voice came that the talisman was not in its usual place, they stole into the room softly, killed the young prince who was sleeping in his crib, cut him into little bits, then laid them in his mother's bed, and gently stained her lips with his blood. Then they called the king, and said, 'See, your beautiful wife is an ogress. She has killed her child in order to eat his flesh.' Then the king was very wroth, and ordered her to be first whipped out of his dominions, and then killed.

So the beautiful Princess Pepperina was scourged out of the kingdom and slain; but when she died her body became a high white wall, her eyes turned into liquid pools of water, her green mantle into stretches of soft grass, her long twining hair into creepers and tendrils, while her scarlet mouth and white teeth changed to a bed of roses and narcissus. Then her soul took the form of *chakwa* and a *chakwi*, and floating on the liquid pools mourned her sad fate all day long.'

Now after many days, the king, who was full of distress for the loss of his young wife, went out hunting, and found no sport anywhere.

By chance he came to the high white wall, and being curious to see what it encircled, he climbed over it, and saw the green grass, and twining tendrils, the roses and narcissus, and the liquid pools with the *chakwa* and *chakwi* floating on them, singing sorrowfully. The king was hot and tired, so he lay down to rest on the grass and listened to the cry of the birds. Then the *chakwa* told his mate the whole story of the wicked women's treachery, and the king listened with a beating heart.

The *chakwi* wept, saying, 'Can she never become alive again?'

'If any one will catch us and hold us close together,' answered the *chakwa*, 'with heart to heart, and then sever our heads from our bodies at one blow, so that neither of us shall die before the other, the Princess Pepperina will take

---

Chakwa and *chakwi*—The ruddy goose or sheldrake, the Brahmani duck. Dr Fallon, *New Hind* Dict., says of this bird:—'It is found all over India in the winter. It breeds on rocks on the borders of the great Himalayan lakes. The bird extends all over central Europe and the greater part of Asia and northern Africa. The Indians have a legend that two lovers for some indiscretion were turned into Brahmani ducks, and condemned to pass the night apart from each other on the opposite banks of a river. All night long each asks the other in turn if it shall join its mate, and the other is always in the negative. Chakwa—Shall I come? No, Chakwi. Chakwi—Shall I come? No, Chakwa.'

her own form again.' The king, delighted at the prospect of seeing his love again, called the *chakwa* and *chakwi* to him: they came quite readily, and stood heart to heart, while he cut off their heads with one blow of his sword. No sooner were their heads off than there stood the Princess Pepperina, smiling and beautiful as ever; but strange to say, the liquid pools and grass, the rose and narcissus remained as they were.

Then said the king, 'Come away home, I will never mistrust you again, and I will kill the wicked traitors who belied you.'

But the Princess said, 'Not so. Let me live here always.'

Just then the jinn woke and yawned. He knew at once by his art where the Princess was, so he flew to her, saying, 'Just so! and here I will live also.'

So he built them a magnificent palace, and there the Princess remained and was happy ever after.

Baludada and Bayobai

Fr. D'Penha

❧

In a certain country there once lived a king, who had one son. The prince was sent to school, where he proved himself worthy of the schoolmaster, and when he had attained maturity, the king, his father, thought it high time to get him married. The prince said to him, 'If you wish to get me married, I shall want a wife who will sustain the dignity of my father and the honour of my mother; else I do not want a wife.'[*]

'Very well,' the king replied, 'we want for nothing, and I will send my messengers to all parts of the country and even to foreign lands to get you just such a wife as you desire.'

Accordingly, he at once despatched people to all parts of the country, and also to foreign courts, with the message: 'If any one has a daughter that will keep up the dignity of the father and the honour of the mother, we wish to enter into an alliance with him.'

'Baludada and Bayobai', from 'Folklore in Salsette' by Geo. Fr. D'Penha. *The Indian Antiquary,* Vol. XX. 1891.

[*] Lit. translation of the son's reply: 'If you wish to get me a wife, get me such a one as will take care of my father's beard and mother's sari, such a wife I want, or I do not want a wife.

The messengers went from village to village and from town to town, and penetrated into foreign countries, but with little success; for who was there that would guarantee to keep up the dignity of the father and the honour of the mother? At length the king of a distant country had an only daughter, and he too received this message, but also refused the proposal. The princess, however, asked her father what the letter contained, but the king refused to tell her. However, after much entreaty she was told what it was about, and exclaimed, 'Yes, father, give them my answer, I will keep up the dignity of the father and the honour of the mother.'

The king, thereupon, sent his own men with another message to the effect that he was willing to enter into the alliance, and that his daughter was willing to fulfil the conditions imposed by the prince. The messengers were also authorized to settle a day for the celebration of the marriage. The messengers reached the prince's dominions, and made all the arrangements necessary, and appointed a day for the auspicious occasion.

Preparations were now made on both sides on a grand scale. Nothing was spared to make the occasion a great event. In due time, on the appointed day, the marriage took place with all possible splendour. The bride was still very young and consequently had to remain at her parent's house till she should attain puberty.

A year or two after the marriage the prince thought of paying a visit to his wife, and expressed his desire to his father. The king, of course, had no objection, and gave his consent, giving him money for his expenses on the way. The prince, however, disguised himself as a poverty-stricken person, and went to his wife's country. When he had arrived there he cut a bundle of grass, and, carrying it on his head, passed by his father-in-law's house. His wife saw him with the grass and called out to him: 'Grasscutter, grasscutter, are you employed or without employment?'

The pretended grasscutter replied, 'I am without employment.'

The princess then said, 'Grasscutter, will you take employment at our house?'

The prince said he was willing to take employment, and was engaged as a servant by his own wife, who, of course, was unaware of the real state of affairs. But the prince knew her, and thought it a fitting opportunity of testing, by observing her behaviour, whether she could fulfil the conditions imposed by him.

This state of things went on for a few years, when one day the parents of the princess called the supposed servant and said to him, 'Grasscutter, we are going to a distant country for a month or two, during which time you must take care of our daughter.'

The servant having promised to take care of the princess, her parents, the king and queen, left for the distant country, and after they were gone the princess one day said to her servant, 'Grasscutter, grasscutter, what is your name?'

The prince replied, 'Baludada,' and asked her in return what her name was, and she answered, 'Bayobai.'

And then she said to him, 'Baludada, would you do anything for me, if I were to tell you to?'

Baludada replied, 'Yes, Bayobai, I will do whatever work you may want me to do.'

And then he said to her, 'Bayobai, you will cook and give me to eat, won't you?'

And Bayobai said, 'Yes, I will give.' And they lived together like brother and sister; Baludada doing whatever he was asked to do, and Bayobai doing the cooking for him.[*]

---

[*] From this point the story runs as that of ordinary person, and not that of a prince and princess, for they are now called Baludada and Bayobai respectively throughout, and the kings and queens are mentioned merely as parents.

About this time Bayobai attained to puberty,[*] that is she was twelve years old, and was one day walking on the sea-beach, when a great merchant arrived with a ship full of pearls and rubies. The merchant spied Bayobai walking on the sea-beach, and was so enamoured of her beauty that he determined at any cost to get hold of her. So he began to enquire in the neighbourhood if it were possible, but the neighbours said that they could not tell, that her parents were not at home, and that she was left under the care of a servant. So he sent for Baludada, and asked him, too, whether he thought his mistress would allow his advances, and promised to give Baludada five hundred rupees, and Bayobai whatever she asked for. Baludada thought this the best opportunity possible of testing her, and went, therefore, running to Bayobai, and said to her, 'Bayobai, will you listen to what I have to say?'

Bayobai said she would, but Baludada again said to her, 'If you agree to what I say, I will tell you.'

Bayobai, little suspecting what the nature of the talk was to be, agreed to do as he should say. Then Baludada told her that a great merchant, who had arrived with a ship full of pearls and rubies, had told him to ask her whether she would admit his advances and to tell her that if she would, he would give her whatever she asked for.

Bayobai upon this said, 'What! Baludada, my parents are not at home, and you tell me such a thing as this!'

Baludada then said that if she did not agree he would leave her service and go away. Upon this Bayobai said, 'Very well, go and tell him that he must give me his word in writing that if I admit him at eight o'clock tonight, and turn him out again as soon as it strikes twelve, I may take his vessel of pearls and rubies.'

---

[*] Twelve years is generally supposed to be the time when a girl attains her puberty and many years ago girls in Salsette were married at that age. The consummation of the marriage, however, did not take place for a few months, and often for the period of a year, though the wife lived in her husband's house.

Baludada immediately went and informed the merchant, and got a document prepared then and there. Then Bayobai sent Baludada to the bazaar to purchase a lot of vegetables, fish, ghee, and such like things, and he went and brought them home. Punctually at eight o'clock that evening the merchant arrived, and Bayobai offered him a seat; and preliminaries being over, she began to cook in order to entertain her guest. She gave Baludada his meal as usual, and asked him to sleep in her house for the night; but he refused to do so, and leaving the house went and hid himself near a window, whence he could watch everything that passed. Now as Bayobai was cooking she wanted a coconut, in searching for which she spent nearly an hour and then another half hour in finding the koita to break the coconut with, and in this way kept on spinning out the time. It was past eleven o'clock by the time she had finished cooking, and then she laid out the supper for the merchant. At supper the merchant was told that he must eat of everything that she might bring, and not rise from the table. Now Bayobai had prepared so many dishes and so many kinds of sweets, which she brought on the table one by one, that before supper was over the clock struck twelve. Upon this Bayobai called out to Baludada in a loud voice, thinking he was asleep in his own hut. Our hero, who was close by, ran off at the first call, and came back running from the direction of his hut, growling, or rather pretending to growl, for having been aroused from sleep, 'What is the matter? Why are you calling me?'

Bayobai then told Baludada to kick the merchant out of the house and appropriate the ship full of pearls and rubies. The poor merchant was compelled to yield, for had he not given a written agreement? He had also, as he had promised, to give five hundred rupees to Baludada.

A month or so after this Bayobai's parents returned from the distant country. Not a word, however, was told to them of what had happened in their absence. Baludada was now perfectly satisfied with Bayobai, for he had tested her under the most trying circumstances, and he thought to himself, 'Bayobai will keep up the dignity of my father and the honour of my mother.'

He had been in his father-in-law's employment for nearly five years, and he now told him that he wished to go home to his parents. So he asked to be paid off for the time he had served, as he had not drawn his pay. Bayobai and her parents had taken such a liking to him that they were very reluctant to let him go, but as he was determined to do so they paid him off and gave him a lot of money over and above what was due to him. Baludada had now plenty of money besides the five hundred rupees he had got from the merchant. He took leave of his friends and returned to his own house.

When he reached his home his parents enquired after his wife, but he stoutly denied his having gone to her, and said he had gone to seek employment, and had returned with a large fortune. How could he have got so much money as he had brought with him, but for the work he had done in all these years?

A few months after this Baludada asked his father to let him go and fetch his wife home, but his father said he would go and bring her himself. So the old man set out one day for his daughter-in-law's (Bayobai's) house, where he was cordially received. After a few days' stay there he told Bayobai's parents that, as she had now attained maturity, he wished to take her home. Her parents said they had no objection, and that they were very happy that he should have come to take her away. Bayobai, therefore, after taking a tender farewell of her parents, set out with her father-in-law, taking with her all the rubies and pearls she had got from the merchant. When they reached home it was late at night and Baludada had by that time gone to sleep, and accordingly Bayobai did not see him. But, for the next few days, Baludada took to his bed and covered himself up from head to food, so that Bayobai had no chance of seeing him. One day, however, Baludada, knowing that Bayobai would go to the well to fetch water, went out and climbed a *bor*[*] tree, and plucking a few ripe *boram*, waited for her on her way to the well. He had not long waited, when Bayobai came up to him, and happy at having seen her servant (for so at least she thought him) after such a long time, addressed him: 'Hallo, Baludada, what are you doing here? Is this your native country? Are you well?'

Baludada replied, 'Yes, Bayobai, this is my country, and I am well.' Baludada then asked Bayobai, 'Bayobai, what are you doing here? Are you well? Have you come to your husband's house? Is your husband well? How are your mother and father-in-law?'

To these questions Bayobai replied, 'Yes, Baludada, I am well enough, and I am come to my husband's house. All are well, but I have not yet seen my husband's face.'

Upon this Baludada said, 'Take a few *boram* and give them to your husband, and then you will have a chance of seeing his face.' And Bayobai answered, 'But, Baludada, my husband won't speak or do anything, and perhaps he would beat me.'

Said Baludada: 'No, he won't beat you.'

Bayobai took the *boram* and went home, and Baludada, going home before her, went to sleep as before.

A few more days passed, and Baludada again went and climbing a mango tree plucked a few ripe mangoes and waited for the arrival of Bayobai. She soon came and Baludada asked her:

'Well, Bayobai, did you give the *boram* to your husband?'

Bayobai answered, 'No, Baludada, I was afraid he might beat me.'

---

[*] Boram (singular, bor) are fruits which ripen about the months of January, February and March. They are both sweet and sour. The tree is also known by the name of bor.

Baludada then gave her the mangoes, saying, 'Do as I tell you. Take these mangoes, and do you know what to do in the night? Take a pair of scissors and cut the cloth off his face and throw him these mangoes. Thus you will see his face and he will be obliged to speak.'

Bayobai again asked, 'But suppose he beats me?'

Baludada then said, 'No, he won't beat you, only do as I tell you.'

And away went Baludada and slept as before.

When she had drawn the water Bayobai went home, and in the night she took a pair of scissors and, as advised by Baludada, cut a piece of the sheet covering him and threw the mangoes on his face. This was too much for Baludada, who could not stifle his laughter, and revealed himself to Bayobai. Bayobai was quite surprised, and asked Baludada why he had played so many tricks. Baludada answered, 'Do you remember that before the wedding I said that I would marry only her who would keep up the dignity of my father and the honour of my mother? It was to find out whether you could really keep the dignity of my father and the honour of my mother, that I played so many tricks.'

They then lived together happily to a good old age.

Suhni and Mehar

C. A. Kincaid

Once upon a time there lived in Guzrat town, on the banks
of the Chenab, a famous potter, named Tallu. His skill in
pottery was famed far and wide and had brought him great
riches. He had born to him in his old age a lovely daughter.
Even as a babe she was so pretty that Tallu gave her the
name of Suhni, or the maiden beautiful.

At the same time there lived in Bokhara a rich
merchant, called Mirza. For all his riches he was unhappy,
because he had no son. One day he heard of a famous fakir
who was reputed to be able to bestow children on the
childless. To him Mirza went and implored his help. 'Of
what use,' he cried bitterly, 'are all my riches, when I have
no son to inherit them?' The fakir pitied the old man, and
said, 'Your wish shall be fulfilled. You shall be blessed with
a son; but beware of the day on which he falls in love!'

Mirza was delighted at the prospect of a son, and paid
but little heed to the fakir's warning. He went back home;
and in less than a year his wife, although well stricken in
years, bore him a son, on exactly the same day as Tallu's
wife in Guzrat gave birth to Suhni.

'Suhni and Mehar', from *Tales of Old Ind* by C. A. Kincaid, 1938.

To the little boy Mirza gave the name of Izat Beg. He grew up, and became a skilled musician and a bold huntsman. But one day a traveller from India came to Bokhara, and, meeting Izat Beg, praised to him so warmly the splendours of Delhi and the greatness of the emperor Shah Jahan, that the youth felt that he must see Delhi or die. He asked his father's leave to go, but Mirza would not hear of it.

Izat Beg was so fired with longing to see the city of the mighty emperor, that he could neither eat nor sleep. At last Mirza, fearing for his son's health, gave him leave to go.

Izat Beg set out with a retinue of servants and a great store of money for the journey, and after some weeks he reached Delhi without mishap. There he gave rich presents to several of the courtiers, and in this way obtained an interview with the emperor. Having feasted his eyes on the pomp and state of the court, Izat Beg thought of returning to Bokhara. As he went homewards, he passed, as his ill fortune willed it, the village of Guzrat. There he heard of Tallu's fame as a potter and he resolved to buy some of Tallu's earthenware as a present for his father. He sent a servant to Tallu; but the man was so dazzled by the beauty of Suhni, whom he saw in her father's shop, that, without buying anything, he ran back to his master, and cried, 'Of the pots I can say nothing, for I had eyes only for the potter's daughter. She is so lovely that she has no earthly rival. No man is fit to wed her save only you, my master.'

Izat Beg was so struck by the man's words that he at once went back with him to Tallu's shop. The moment he saw Suhni, he, too, lost all thought of buying Tallu's pots. All he could do was to gaze, distracted with love, on the potter's daughter. To be the longer with her, he made her show him every pot in Tallu's shop, feigning not to be pleased with any of them. At last Suhni lost all patience with him, and said, 'Young sir, if you wish to buy my father's pots, buy them; but if not, pray excuse me, as I have other work waiting for me.'

Izat Beg, sooner than displease her, bought all the costliest earthenware she had, and went back to his camp. But he had fallen so deeply in love with Suhni that he could not bear to leave Guzrat. He opened a shop in the town and stocked it with Tallu's pottery. Each day he went to Tallu's shop and bought pots at any price the potter asked, and, taking them to his shop, sold them for anything the villagers chose to offer him. In this way he soon spent the greater part of his money. His servants, who wished to go back to their homes, began to fear that they would never see Bokhara again. Taking counsel together, they one night robbed their master of such money as he still had, and with it went back to their native country.

Next morning the unhappy Izat Beg woke to find himself a beggar. For some time he went daily to Tallu's shop and bought pots on credit, promising to pay their price later. But at last Tallu refused to sell him any more and pressed him for payment. Izat Beg pleaded that his servants had robbed him; at the same time he offered to work for Tallu, and so pay off his debt. Tallu agreed, and made him sweep the house daily and fetch clay for his earthenware from the river bed.

Izat Beg, fearing that he might be sent away, worked so hard that in the end he fell ill. Tallu, taking pity on him, sent him to graze the buffaloes, that he might regain his strength; and as he did not know his real name, he called him Mehar or herdsman.

One day, as Mehar grazed his buffaloes, Suhni came up to him and asked him to give her some milk. Izat Beg consented, and, as he milked a she-buffalo, he told her his story, how he was the son of a rich merchant of Bokhara, how he had given up all his wealth and his home, his parents and his country, all for love of her. As Suhni heard his tale and saw what a goodly youth he was, tears rolled down her cheeks, and before he had done, she was as much in love with him as he with her.

Every day thereafter Suhni would meet Mehar, and, feigning to beg milk of him, would pass an hour or more in his company. At last the village tongues began to wag, and everyone whispered to his neighbour that Tallu's daughter loved the buffalo-herd. The talk reached Tallu's ears, and in great wrath he drove Mehar out of Guzrat. Then, in spite of her tears and entreaties, he married Suhni to her cousin, who lived close by. But when the wedding night came, Suhni prayed to Allah to save her from the clutches of her husband whom she hated; and Allah, taking pity on her, wrapped him night after night in so deep a sleep that he never thought of the fair girl by his side.

Now Mehar, driven out of Guzrat, went to live across the Chenab, so that he might still see by day the roof to the potter's house, beneath which lived his beloved. He bore their separation well enough until he heard of her marriage to her cousin. Then, beside himself with jealousy and grief, he wrote her a bitter letter, taunting her with her faithlessness to one who had given up all for her. His cruel words pierced Suhni to the heart. She wrote back begging him to meet her that night on the river-bank near her husband's house, and promising that she would show him that she loved him still.

The letter gave new life to Mehar. That night he swam across the Chenab, and met Suhni on the river-bank. There, while her husband slept in the deathlike sleep sent him by Allah, Suhni and Mehar passed many happy hours. They supped off a fish that Mehar had bought off a fisherman as a present for Suhni, and before the eastern sky grew light, Mehar swam back to his hiding-place across the Chenab.

The next night, and many nights afterwards, he swam the dark waters to meet his beloved. Always he brought with him a freshly caught fish, that they might sup together, while her husband slept.

One day, however, there had been a strong wind, and

the fishermen had caught no fish. Fearing Suhni might think that he had grown miserly, or that his love for her was waning, Mehar cut a piece of flesh off his thigh, intending to pass it off as a fish that he had bought for her. When he reached the opposite bank, he was so weak with pain that he fainted. Suhni, seeing the blood streaming down his leg, tended his wound. In reply to her questions, he told her what he had done. Tenderly reproaching him, she tied up the wound, and forbade him to swim across the river again. She promised she would swim across to him in future. That night Mehar, wounded though he was, struggled safely back across the river.

Next day Suhni took a seasoned jar from her father's house, and, when night fell, swam boldly out into the Chenab with the jar under her. The night was dark and stormy, but the jar bore her up; and with strong, swift strokes she crossed the river, and found Mehar on the bank, ready to clasp her to his bosom. Before morning came, she had swum back and was fast asleep in her husband's house.

Thus, night after night, Suhni crossed and recrossed the Chenab, borne up by the earthen vessel beneath her. Unhappily, one night, her husband's sister saw Suhni leave her house and, jar in hand, go to the riverside. She followed Suhni, and saw her swim across the river and after some hours swim back again. Furious for her brother's sake, she vowed that she would rid him of so unfaithful a wife. She noted where Suhni hid her jar, and then went quietly home. But at noon she took an unseasoned pot, and put it in place of the one that had so often carried Suhni across the stream.

When darkness came, Suhni fetched, as she thought, the jar that she had hidden, and went to the edge of the river. The rain was pouring in torrents, and the waters roared as if warning her not to go. But trusting in the vessel that had so often carried her, she swam out, as before, into the raging torrent. When she reached midstream, the unseasoned jar crumbled to pieces beneath her, and without its help Suhni could not battle against the current. She struggled bravely for a time, then wearied and sank.

All that night Mehar waited in vain for Suhni on the farther bank. When morning broke, he knew that she must have perished in the cruel water. Life without her, for whom he had given up his home and country, seemed to him worthless. With a great cry to Suhni that he was coming, he sprang into the river and was never seen again.

Hir and Ranjho

C. A. Kincaid

Once upon a time a king, named Chuchak, ruled at Jhang Sayal, on the banks of the Chenab river. He had a beautiful daughter, called Hir: her neck was like a swan's, her eyes were like a deer's, and her voice like a koel's. Nor was she only beautiful to look upon: she was also a mine of wit and wisdom. Her father had built her a palace on the banks of the Chenab river, but he did not force her to live in it, as if in a prison. He had a beautiful boat built for her, and in it she would take long trips up and down the river; at night the dwellers on the banks would hear her singing in her cabin, like a nightingale in its cage.

At the same time, in the Hazara country, there ruled four princes, all sons of the same father: of the four the bravest and the most beloved was prince Ranjho. One day there came to prince Ranjho's palace a traveller. The prince received him courteously and hospitably. Noticing that the traveller was preoccupied and sad, the prince asked him what ailed him. 'Nothing ails me, my lord prince,' replied the traveller, 'but my thoughts are far away in my own city of Jhang Sayal. Over it rules king Chuchak, and there too dwells his daughter Hir, whose beauty I cannot describe, so wonderful it is. If I seem sad and my thoughts wander, it is because I, like all the noble youths of our city, am in love with her. Indeed, it was to gain peace of mind that I set out on my travels.'

The prince's fancy was fired by the tale, and he begged the traveller to describe princess Hir, however imperfectly. The traveller consented; and so glowing was his tale and so passionate his words, that the prince sprang to his feet. 'Promise me that I shall see her,' he cried, 'or I will kill myself before your eyes.' 'There is no need to die,' said the traveller soothingly, 'send an envoy to her father's palace and ask for her hand in marriage.'

Prince Ranjho did not send the envoy, for he feared to court a refusal. Nevertheless the image, so deftly painted by the traveller, danced always before his eyes, and he lost all power to eat or sleep. His brothers, seeing his pitiable state, conspired against him, drove him out of the kingdom, and divided his inheritance.

The unhappy Ranjho could think of no better plan than to beg his way to the country of her for love of whom he had lost his kingdom. The way was long from Hazara to Jhang Sayal, and the prince was half dead of fatigue before he came to the Chenab river. At last he saw it in the distance, and on its banks the palace of the princess Hir. Opposite the palace was moored the princess's boat. The prince called to the boatman, who stood on the deck, 'I have come from a far country and I am very weary. Pray, let me rest in yonder boat.' The boatman turned, and seeing a tall and gallant youth, guessed him to be of noble birth. Very courteously he answered, 'Young lord, that boat is the princess Hir's; I cannot let you go on board.'

Prince Ranjho walked towards the boat, hoping to be able to persuade the boatman to let him see the princess. When he reached the water's edge, his worn-out limbs gave way and he fell headlong into the river. The kindly boatman would not let him drown, and, rowing to where the prince was struggling against the current, dragged him into the boat, and let him rest himself in the princess's cabin. A moment later the prince was fast asleep.

It so happened that Hir resolved that day to go sailing on the river earlier than was her wont. With sixty serving maids she walked across the garden that stretched between her palace and the river. When the boatman saw her coming he began to tremble. He called to his wife and said, 'Go and appease the princess, or, when she sees this stranger in her cabin, she will have me flayed alive.' His wife left the boat and began to scream at the top of her voice. The princess heard her and, running towards her, asked what was the matter. 'O lady, forgive my husband!' sobbed the boatman's wife. 'A young man has forced his way into your cabin and is fast asleep on your bed!' When the princess heard these words, her eyes blazed with anger. 'How dare he?' she cried. 'Where is he? I will kill him.' She ran into the cabin, meaning to stab the stranger to the heart, but when her gaze fell on the sleeping youth, her anger vanished. As she drank in the beauty of the prince, he slowly opened his eyes and, to his surprise, saw before him a maid fairer than the fairies themselves; her eyes were like lotuses, her shape beggared all description. Hir, as if fascinated, came slowly to the side of the cot. The prince held out his arms, and a moment later their lips met.

Hir would not let the prince rise, but, sitting by his side, made him tell her who he was and whence he had come. He told her; and her eyes filled with tears, that he should have lost a kingdom for love of her. Then she said, 'Lord of my heart, you cannot stay here in my cabin. Our secret will soon spread abroad. My father will hear of it and will kill you.' She thought for some time, and then said, 'There is only one way that I can think of, and that is for you to put on a disguise and hire yourself as a buffalo-herd to my father. You can then graze his buffaloes along the river, and

I can meet you daily.' The prince laughingly consented, and dressed himself as a buffalo-herd in the clothes that Hir procured for him. After bidding him a tender farewell, the princess went to her mother, the queen, and said to her, 'Our buffaloes are not thriving. They need a skilled herdsman to look after them. I have seen a herdsman from Hazara, who, so I have heard, has great knowledge of cattle. Let us hire him, and our buffaloes will grow fat.' Her mother agreed; and when Ranjho later in the day offered himself for hire, she ordered a thousand buffaloes to be given into his care.

No one was then so happy as the princess. Daily she would slip down the river in her boat, and, meeting Ranjho, would spend the day with him in the shade of some tree on the river's edge.

But, in spite of all her care, her love for Ranjho got noised abroad, and men began to whisper: 'The princess Hir has lost her honour to a cowherd!' The rumour at last reached the ears of Hedo, the brother of the queen, and he told his sister. The queen sent for the princess and charged her with her guilt. At first Hir denied the story as mere lying gossip, but at last she told her mother everything. The queen was beside herself with anger, and cried, 'Unless you promise to give up this vile cowherd, whom you forsooth dub a prince, I will tell the king, and he will surely put you both to death.' Hir shook her head sadly and said, 'My mother, I can make no such promise. I have given my life into another's keeping. If I give him up, I give my life up also.' Then the queen rose and brought king Chuchak. When the king heard what his daughter had done, he drew his sword and would have killed her, but at the queen's entreaty he sent her to prison instead. Then he bade his guards beat Ranjho and drive him from the city.

Half killed, the unhappy prince dragged himself to a wood at some distance from Jhang Sayal and there he lived, sustained only by the hope that he might again see the princess. Nor did the hope prove vain. The princess pined so in her prison cell, that the queen prevailed on king Chuchak to release her. No sooner was she free, than she made her way to the wood where prince Ranjho was, and fell weeping into his arms. She stayed with him for a short time and then returned to her palace; but every evening she would slip out and take food and drink to Ranjho.

Now Hir's uncle, Hedo, kept a watch on his niece, and, disguised in a beggar's clothes, he followed her to the wood. Returning he told the king what he had seen. King Chuchak, seeing Hir's great love for Ranjho, would have joined them in marriage, but his sons would not hear of it. First they tried to kill prince Ranjho in his lair in the woods: but although he was one to four, he beat them off, until at last they ran away screaming for their lives. Then they formed another plan. They went to the court of king Norang of Norangpur and offered Hir in wedlock to king Norang's son, Khiro. Prince Khiro gladly accepted the princess's hand, and the four princes returned to Jhang Sayal and bade their sister make ready for her marriage. But Hir refused to make any preparations; and when her ladies came to put henna on her, as befitted a bride-to-be, she drove them out of the room.

The king in despair took his daughter to the kazi. The kazi at first spoke softly to her. 'My child,' he said, 'you should not love a stranger of whom your parents know nothing. You should only love him of whom your parents approve.' But Hir would not be cajoled. She stamped her foot and said, 'What do you know about love, kazi? If I have drunk the cup of love without my parents' knowledge, I at least know what the cup contains.' Then the kazi grew angry and said, 'You are a wicked girl; you have committed a great sin. To disobey your parents is to transgress the scriptures.' So saying, he took out his holy books, and would have read her passages from them, but Hir stormed at him: 'A plague,' she cried, 'on your scrawls and your zigzags! I do not know a *zabar*[*] from a *zer*! What care I if *alif* stands for Allah or *mim* for Mahomed or *ain* for Ali! Your holy books, you say, have come from heaven, but you cannot show me any passage in them that prescribes rules for love: yet love is as old as Adam! Why should a lover need books, when the mirror in his heart shows him the form of his beloved?' The kazi, when he heard this bold reply, foamed at the mouth with rage. 'Take her away,' he screamed. 'Take her away and kill her; she is not fit to live!' The king took her away but he did not kill her. He sent her to Norangpur, where, sore against her will, she was married to prince Khiro.

In the meantime prince Ranjho donned the garb of a fakir, and went on foot to Norangpur. Passing close to Hir's window he contrived, with the help of her sister-in-law Sahti, to make his presence in the town known to her. The same day Hir cried out that a cobra had bitten her in the foot; and, falling on the ground, she feigned to be in agony. The court-doctors were sent for, but they could do nothing. At last Sahti suggested that the fakir who had just come to Norangpur might perhaps effect a cure. The fakir was sent for, and at once promised to cure the princess, provided that he and she were left alone together. The others left them, and Hir and Ranjho embraced. Hir promised her lover to leave the palace and run away with him that very night. Then, to soothe the suspicions of her companions, he began to recite mantras loudly enough for those outside to hear. In a short time the fakir went out of the room and pronounced the princess cured; and, calling in her companions, he claimed, and received, a rich reward.

That night the princess slipped unseen out of the palace; and, joining Ranjho outside the walls of Norangpur, she fled with him towards Hazara. In vain king Norang sent horsemen to catch them; for, thinking that the fugitives

---

[*] 'Zabar' is the sign for the vowel 'a' and 'zer' the sign for the vowel 'i'.

must be fleeing to Jhang Sayal, the horsemen took the wrong road and so never caught up with them.

After great toil and hardships, Ranjho and Hir reached Hazara. There Ranjho's brothers had ruled so ill and harshly, that when the people saw their favourite prince again, they rose in thousands, and, putting the prince at their head, stormed the palace and drove his three brothers from Hazara, just as formerly they themselves had driven out the prince. In this way Ranjho became master of his father's entire kingdom. He married the princess Hir and made her his queen, and together they ruled over the people of Hazara for many years afterwards.

Umar and Marai

C. A. Kincaid

❧

Once upon a time there ruled in Umarkot a famous king called Umar. He was a Rajput of the Sumro clan, and such was the splendour of his reign, that it would have restored their sight to the blind. Whether in the chase or in battle, he was as brave as a lion; and the justice of his rule was famous far and wide.

But all men, high or low, bad or good, rich or poor, must fulfil their destiny. Thus it came about that one day king Umar sat in his hall of audience, surrounded by his officers and governors, and to all of them he gave a solemn warning that they should fear God and oppress no man. Suddenly, in front of the palace-gate, a stranger cried out that he craved a private audience with the king, as he had a message for his ears alone. When the king heard this, he dismissed his officers and governors, and received the stranger.

Now at the time that king Umar reigned at Umarkot, there lived in a village called Malir, in the Thar desert, a humble goatherd, named Palvi. He had a wife, named Merad, and a lovely daughter, called Marai. In their house

'Umar and Marai' from *Tales of Old Ind* by C. A. Kincaid, 1938.

also lived a servant, Phog by name, who aspired to Marai's hand. But Palvi had promised his daughter to her cousin Khet, whom she loved. So he rejected Phog's suit. In a fury, Phog left Malir, and thirsting for vengeance, went to the palace-gate at Umarkot: he was the stranger who asked for, and obtained, an audience of king Umar.

When Phog was alone with the king, he said, 'My lord king, I have a humble petition to make; and it is this. There lives in Malir a maiden, called Marai, whose beauty puts the sun to shame. Her form is tall and straight; her eyes are blacker than the humming bees, her glances sharper than a soldier's sword; her skin is like satin; when she smiles, it is as if there fell a shower of pearls; her bosom is as white as the clouds in spring, and the buds there put to shame the rosebuds in your garden; her face is fairer than the moonbeam; her gait is like the pea-hen's, and when she speaks the koels answer her from the forest. When a man has once seen her, he can look at naught else: yet she is but a goatherd's daughter, and in rags. If she were clad in fine raiment, she would be fairer than the *paris*. Only you, O king, are fit to possess her. For if her form is lovely, her heart is a treasure-house of love. Come with me, and I will show you where she lives.'

King Umar forgot all the noble words that he had just spoken to his officers and governors, and went mad with love for the goatherd's beautiful daughter. He had his fastest camel saddled, and, taking the reins, he mounted in front, while the treacherous servant sat behind him and showed him the way to Marai's village.

It so happened that Marai had gone with a girl-companion to fetch water at a well outside her village. Seeing a camel with two men riding upon it in the distance, she grew frightened and would have run back to her home, but the girl with her, curious to see the strangers, told her not to be afraid. 'They are travellers,' she said, 'they will do you no harm. When they come to the well, they will ask for water. We will give it to them, and in return they will tell us all the news.' Marai, persuaded by her companion, went on with her to the well, and reached it at the same time as Umar's camel. Phog's whisper and king Umar's own eyes told him that it was the beautiful Marai who stood before him. He made his camel kneel, and alighting asked Marai for water. The simple girl was preparing to give him some, when suddenly Umar and Phog seized her and gagged her, and, tying her on the camel's back, took her away with them to the palace at Umarkot.

That night king Umar went to Marai and found her weeping. Her food lay untouched by her side. He tried to console her, saying, 'Marai, do not weep. What is done, cannot be undone. You shall be my chief queen, and my other queens shall be your slaves. In your hands I will put the reins of my kingdom.' But Marai only wept the more, as she thought of her home, of her parents, and of Khet, her affianced lover. Then king Umar said scornfully, 'Why should you grieve for your parents and your lover, Marai? They are wild foresters. Here your word will be law to princes. In your village you have to rise at dawn and drive the goats in the sun; here you will live shaded and sheltered under the roof of my pallace.'

'Your ladies,' retorted Marai, 'think that it is a great thing to veil their faces and live behind palace-walls. But I love the open air and the sunshine on my face. I love the feel of a kid under each arm, as I go with the goats to the grazing-ground. I have nothing in common with your high-born beauties. They like dainty food; I live on wild fruit and berries. They have jewels round their necks; I wear a string of red beads. They love soft beds and bedding; I love to stretch out on the cool sand. In their courtyards servants scatter water to settle the dust, but I love to feel the raindrops. They wear silk clothes; I wear coarse rags. They listen to the sound of your fifes and drums, but far sweeter to my ears is the bleating of my goats.'

'But I will make you the fairest garden in all the world,' said king Umar. 'It shall be hung with gold lamps, and in it will grow vines and dates, plantains and limes, figs and oranges, cocoa-nuts and almonds; and the air will be heavy with the scent of areca-nut, cardamoms, and sandalwood.'

Marai shook her head, and answered, 'Nay, keep those for others, king Umar. Give me back the rough uplands that stretch round my village, and the brambles and thorn-bushes on the hills, and the fruit and wild berries that grow on them.'

For many a night king Umar tried in vain to win Marai's love, but she was proof alike against tears, threats, and entreaties. One day he pitched a tent some miles from Umarkot, and bade herdsmen graze their cattle and goats round it, so that the sight of it might soften Marai's heart and make her smile on him. But Marai only laughed scornfully, and said, 'Your trouble is wasted. The goats are like my village-goats, and the tent is like the tents in my village; but in the tent you should have put my parents, and the goatherd should have been my lover, Khet.'

Then king Umar sent for a camel-man and bade him dress himself like a Malir peasant. Next he sent word to Marai that a man had come from her village with a message from her parents; and he asked leave to bring him to her room. Marai consented. When the man entered the room, he said, 'Your mother has sent me to you. Listen to her message, for these are her very words: "My daughter, why do you bring on us the hatred of king Umar by your obstinacy? All the world knows that he has taken you to his palace. Even though you remain chaste, the world will think you unchaste, so why refuse his love?"' But Marai guessed the trick, and as she looked sternly at the false messenger he faltered and stammered beneath her gaze. 'Love!' she repeated angrily. 'There is no love but that blessed by heaven. No parents of mine would have sent me such a message. It is a black lie, which you have been bribed to tell me.' When this scheme failed, king Umar strode out of the palace in a rage, vowing vengeance against Marai's parents and her lover; but for some time he left her in peace.

In the meantime Marai's parents had heard from her girl-companion how she had been carried off; but when they learnt later that the wrongdoer was no other than the great king Umar of Umarkot, they did nothing to rescue her. They fancied that her heart had yielded to the passion of the king and to the glamour of a royal palace.

But Marai's lover, Khet, distracted by her loss, went on foot to Umarkot and daily wandered in despair around her dwelling. Marai saw him from her window and contrived to send him a message to be at a well-known shrine on a certain day with a swift camel. The next time king Umar came to see Marai, she soothed him by promising that if her parents and clansmen did not rescue her within twelve months of her capture, she would be his. By such soft words she got from him leave to visit the shrine on the day when Khet was to meet her. On the appointed day she and a crowd of richly dressed girl-companions went together to worship at the shrine. When they reached it, they got down from their *palkis*, and laughing and chattering and admiring each other's jewels, they paid little heed to a poorly dressed camel-man who stood by a kneeling camel, not far from the saint's tomb. Suddenly, as they passed him, Marai left the group of heedless girls and ran to the kneeling camel as fast as she could. In a moment she and the camel-man, who was her lover, Khet, had jumped on its back, and the camel, rising to its feet, was soon racing towards Malir. The girls cried after her, 'What are you doing, Marai? Why are you riding off with a stranger on a camel?' Marai called back mockingly, 'Tell king Umar that on a camel I came, and on a camel I went.'

The girls went back to their *palkis*, and, going home, told king Umar with trembling lips what had happened. The king was afraid to send an army into the desert to fetch

Marai back, lest his nobles might upbraid him for doing injustice, when he bade others be just. So Marai reached her home safely. There she married her cousin Khet. Neither king Umar nor the wicked Phog ever came to trouble them again, and they lived happily ever after.

Momul and Rano

C. A. Kincaid

Once upon a time there lived in Sind a king, Nanda by name. He had a wonderful pig's tooth which had the power of drying up water if put close to it. King Nanda used the pig's tooth in this way: he took it to the Indus, and putting the tooth close to the surface of the water, dried up the great river. Whenever king Nanda wanted money, he would go to the bank of the Indus and dry it up with his magical tooth, take from it such treasure as he needed, and return home. When he took the pig's tooth away, the river began to flow once more.

Now it so happened that an anchorite learnt about the pig's tooth by means of his inner knowledge. Filled with greed, he went to the king's palace when Nanda was absent. King Nanda had nine daughters, of whom Momul was the most beautiful, and the wisest, Somal. When the anchorite reached the palace, he began to weep and moan and groan so loudly that his cries roused the princesses. Unhappily the wise Somal, who would have seen through the anchorite's pretence, had gone away with king Nanda. As it was, the beautiful Momul sent for the anchorite and

'Momul and Rano', from *Tales of Old Ind* by C. A. Kincaid, 1938.

asked him what ailed him. He told her that he was very ill and dying, but could he but get a pig's tooth, he would at once get well. Momul remembered that her father, the king, had a pig's tooth. Not knowing its magical properties, she took it from Nanda's room and gave it to the stranger. The anchorite took it and instantly recovered from his feigned illness. Then, going to the bank of the Indus, he dried up its waters, dug out a treasure, and travelling to a distant city spent the rest of his life there, in great peace and happiness.

When king Nanda came back with his daughter Somal and learnt that Momul had given his pig's tooth to a wandering anchorite, he was so angry that he would have killed Momul, had not his wise daughter Somal soothed him by saying that she knew a way in which Momul could get back just as big a treasure as the anchorite had stolen. Next day she took Momul to a spot far out on the Sind *pat* or desert, and there by her sorcery she created a beautiful palace and round it a garden blooming with flowers, and fragrant with fruit. In front of the garden she laid out a maze, round which there seemed to flow a great red river, which she named the Kak. Leading into the maze was a tunnel. Inside the tunnel Somal put by means of her sorcery terrible contrivances which roared and screamed at her will. At each corner of the magic palace she chained a lion, ready to tear into pieces any one who sought to enter. When her task was done, she called Momul, and bade her and her slave-girls live in the palace and proclaim that she would wed the first man who could find his way through the tunnel and maze to her chamber.

Now such was Momul's beauty that all the princes and nobles of Sind, taking with them their treasure and their men-servants, went forth gaily to win the lovely princess. As the wooers came to the outer gate, Momul sent her slave-girls to greet them and invite them to try to win her hand. Led by the slave-girls, one by one they entered the tunnel and passed into the maze. Then the magic river Kak circled round the maze, closing all exits, so that the wooers died miserably, one after the other, and the princess's slaves stripped their bodies and plundered their treasure. A few only, whose hearts failed them in the tunnel or who fled back from the maze before the Kak river surrounded it, wholly escaped; but they found that in their absence Momul's slaves had taken their tents and their horses.

Now about this time there ruled in Umatkot king Hamir, a Rajput of the Sumro clan. He had three viziers, all devoted to one another and still more to king Hamir. Nor would the king ever go hunting or to battle unless either Dunar or Shinro or Rano rode at his side. All four were as handsome and brave as could be, but the handsomest and bravest was Rano.

One day the king and his viziers went a-hunting. As they came to a village, they saw a beggar-man standing by the road-side. His face and bearing were those of a man gently born, but he was covered with rags and half-dead with want and wretchedness. At first the four young men laughed at his strange appearance. Then they went up to him and asked him who he was and whence he came. 'You seem to be gently born,' said king Hamir, 'yet I have never seen anyone in such a sorry state.' The beggar answered courteously, 'My lord king, there was a time when I was rich as any one of the three nobles with you. I had horses and lands and a host of attendants. But one day, to my sorrow, I heard of the beauty of princess Momul, and with a great store of gold and a troop of companions I set forth to win her. But she and her slaves murdered all my friends and plundered me even of my horse, so that I am now begging my way back to my own country.'

The king asked who Momul was, and the beggar-man told her story. After hearing it, the king and his three viziers vowed that they too would try to win her, or would die in the attempt. They asked the beggar-man the way to

her palace, and after several days' journey they reached the
outer gate of her garden, just as it was growing dark. They
camped there for the night, and next morning one of
Momul's slave-girls came to greet them. Here name was
Natar, and she was so pretty and graceful that at first the
four young men thought that she must be Momul herself.
But Natar laughed, and said, 'Nay, I am not the princess.
To see her, you must win through to the palace. No man
except her father has yet seen her face. But she sent me to
welcome you and offer you this tray of food.' She put down
the tray on the ground; and as the young men ate the food,
she described to them Momul's beauty, until they all grew
sick with love. Then she mocked them, saying, 'Who are you
to think of my lovely princess? The hero who would win her
must be cast in a different mould. You had better run back
to your villages. If not, you will be torn to pieces in the
tunnel, or die of hunger and thirst in her maze.' In this way
Natar excited their desire and their courage, until they all
cried together that they feared neither the tunnel nor the
maze, but that they would stay by Momul's gate until they
bore off in triumph the beautiful maiden. In answer, the
slave-girl threw them a tangled skein of silk and said, 'Test
your skill by undoing this, before you try to find your way
through the maze.' King Hamir took the skein; first he, and
then Dunar, and then Shinro tried in vain to unravel it. At
last they passed it on to Rano. His deft fingers soon solved
the knot, and untying it he made the silken skein into a
tassel and fastened it as a plume to his horse's head.

The slave-girl looked at Rano in wonder; then she went
back to her mistress, and said, 'Four beautiful youths have
come to win you, but one, Rano by name, is fairer and wiser
than the others, or indeed than any wooer who has yet come
to your palace-door. Why not marry him, my mistress, at
once? Do not kill this gallant as you have killed the others.'
The princess felt a moment's pity. Then she hardened her
heart and answered, 'If, forsooth, he is as wise as you say,

let him win me. If he fails, he is but a fool, and I shall add his wealth to my father's treasure.'

Then she got ready some tasty dishes, and put a deadly poison in each of them. Giving them to the slave-girl, she bade her take them back to the king and his three viziers. The slave-girl did so; and setting the tray before them, served each of them with her own hands, saying, 'Fair sirs, my mistress has cooked these dishes with her own hands for you as she fears that you must be weary after trying to unravel the skein.' The king and Shinro and Dunar would have eaten the food and perished miserably, had not Rano thrown a piece to a stray dog. The dog ate is, and at once rolled over screaming in agony. The king rose in wrath and said to his viziers, 'We will go back to our homes and let this murderess be.' But Rano replied, 'O king, to go back now would be the act of cowards. Let us go on with our task; and, with God's help, we shall win the maiden.'

In the meantime, Natar went back to the palace and told Momul how Rano had saved his comrades from the poison. She again pleaded with her mistress to spare him. But the princess rebuked her, saying, 'If I spared him, all men would laugh at me. Go now to the young men, and invite them, one by one, to win through to my chamber. When they have entered the maze, they will fall easy victims.'

Natar did as her mistress ordered. Going to king Hamir, she said, 'Come with me, king Hamir. My princess challenges you to win her. If you but find your way to her chamber, she is yours.'

The king rose to his feet and followed the slave-girl into the tunnel. There, in the darkness, she slipped away, leaving the king alone. The contrivances created by Somal's magic began to roar and scream, imitating the cries of wild beasts and the hissing of snakes, and filling the whole air with horror. The king all but fainted. Had he fainted outright, he would have been lost; for the princess's slaves were lurking near, and they would have fallen on him and killed and robbed him. But he recovered himself; and giving up the quest, made his way back to where his comrades sat waiting. He told them of the horrors of the tunnel and of the awful noises that he had heard there. 'Let us stay here no longer,' he said to his viziers. 'Let us go back to Umarkot.'

But Rano said: 'My lord king, although you have failed, you have tried; and so none can blame you. But if we go back without even trying, all Umarkot will laugh us to scorn. Let us all try. Then if we fail, we can go back together.'

Just then Natar came to the camp, and said with a mocking smile. 'You stayed in the princess's garden but a short time, king Hamir. You will never win Momul thus. Now, who among your viziers will come with me to seek her?'

Dunar rose and mounted his horse and followed Natar into the tunnel. There she slipped away; and all round Dunar, Somal's contrivances began to hiss and roar and scream. Dunar's heart failed him, and turning his horse's head, he galloped back trembling to the king's camp, and told his comrades what had befallen him.

A few minutes later, Natar came out of the garden and said scornfully, 'King Hamir, your vizier stayed on the quest even less time than you did. Hearts so faint will never win so fair a lady.'

Then Shinro rose and donned his armour; and mounting a chestnut horse, he followed Natar into the tunnel. But he too lost heart, and galloped back before entering the maze.

At last Rano rose to try his fortune. While the others in vain sought to dissuade him, Natar came to the camp; and her lips curled with scorn, as she said, 'It is but waste of time to lead you into my mistress's garden. You are all cowards, impostors! At the first sound you run away like frightened hares. Such cravens will never win Momul and her beauty.'

Rano donned his armour and mounted a dun horse and praying to Heaven to help him, he followed Natar into the tunnel. There he seized her, so that she should not leave him, and he held her firmly, while Momul's hellish machine roared and screamed all round him, until his ears were deafened with the noise and his eyes blinded with the darkness. The cunning slave-girl, finding that she could not free herself, led Rano to the edge of a pit. There she gave his horse a push, so that it fell into the pit, carrying its rider with it. As Rano fell, he heard the slave-girl laugh scornfully at him out of the darkness.

Happily, the horse fell under the youth, so that he was not badly hurt by the fall. He clambered out, and made his way from the tunnel into the maze. As soon as Rano was inside the maze, the waters of the Kak river closed round it, so that whenever he came to the edge of the maze, he found a raging torrent in front of him. To test its force, he threw into it an areca-nut. But the nut, instead of floating, bounded along the surface of the stream. Then Rano guessed that the Kak river was but an illusion, and that the ground in front of him was only part of the dry desert. So he walked to the edge of the river, and stepped boldly into it. At once the river vanished; and Rano, walking on, found himself close to Momul's palace.

The lions in the palace-courtyard crouched as if to spring on the youth, while, from the window, the princess screamed and scolded at him. But drawing his sword, he rushed past the lions and through the palace-door. Then he ran upstairs into the room where he had seen the princess. She no longer screamed or scolded. Directly he entered the room, she ran towards him and threw herself into his ams, crying, 'You have won me fairly, bold prince! Take me! I am yours.'

II

When morning broke, Rano took leave of the princess. At first Momul would not hear of his going. Indeed, it was not until he had promised to return every night, that, with many tears and embraces, she let her lover go. He put on his armour, mounted his dun horse, and rode back through the maze and the tunnel until he reached king Hamir's camp. There a cry of joy greeted him from Hamir and his two viziers, for they had been grieving for him as for one dead. 'Where have you been?' 'Why did you tarry so long?' 'Did you win your way to the magic palace?' Such were the questions that met him on his return.

Rano feared the king's jealous wrath; so he answered with downcast eyes that he too had failed. 'All night,' he said, 'I wandered in that accursed tunnel, and only now I have escaped.'

Shinro and Dunar believed him; but the king suspected Rano's words to be false, for his bearing was not that of a man who had failed in a high adventure. 'My comrades,' said the king, 'as we have all failed, let us go back to Umarkot; but let none of us say aught to any man, or the shame of our failure will resound throughout India.'

The king and his three viziers rode back silently to Umarkot; for Hamir was angry with Rano, Shinro and Dunar were sad at their ill success, and Rano feared the wrath of his master.

On reaching Umarkot, Rano at once bethought himself of his promise to Momul. That very night, and every night afterwards, Rano mounted a wonderful she-camel that he had, and in an hour's time she brought him from Umarkot to the princess's palace. Before dawn, he rose and bade Momul good-bye; before daylight, he was back in his own house. This he did night after night for several weeks; but all the time the king's anger was burning more and more fiercely, until at last he refused to speak to Rano or acknowledge his salute, and he thought only how he might bring about Rano's ruin.

At last Rano sought a private audience of the king. He confessed to him that he had lied, and begged his mercy. 'Tell me what really happened,' said king Hamir, 'and I will forgive you.' Rano told the king the whole truth; how he had won through the tunnel and the maze, how he had crossed the magic river, and how, sword in hand, he had forced his way into Momul's room. Then he described the beauty of Momul with such glowing words, that king Hamir longed to see her more than ever. 'Let me see her but once,' he cried, 'and I will give back to you all my former favour.'

Rano thought for a moment; then he said, 'She will not see you, king Hamir, if you come as a king. But if you come disguised as my servant, she will suspect nothing, and you will see her.'

So king Hamir disguised himself as a cowherd. He put on an old garment that reached his feet, he tied a scarf round his head, and he took a stick in his hand. Then he got up behind Rano on his swift camel, and in an hour's time they had reached the outer gate of Momul's garden. Rano guided the camel through the tunnel and the maze, across the river, and into Momul's courtyard. There he made the camel kneel, and flinging the nose-string to king Hamir, he walked into the palace and up the stairs into Momul's room. Momul asked who the man was whom he had brought with him. 'He is only a cowherd,' said Rano. But Momul answered, 'If he is only a cowherd, how comes it that he is so fair?' 'He is the son of a slave-girl,' said Rano, 'and he was brought up in my father's house.' But Momul suspected that the stranger was no herdsman. To test him, she had a she-buffalo brought into the courtyard and bade him milk it. Then she turned into the palace with Rano, and both forgot all else but each other's love.

King Hamir milked the she-buffalo as best he could, but his body itched and his hands grew red with the unwonted labour, and all the time his wrath grew fiercer against Rano, whom he knew to be in the arms of the lovely woman who had spoken to him so curtly. Every minute seemed a month, until at last his growlings and cursings reached the ears of Rano upstairs. He rose and, bidding Momul farewell, went back to the courtyard and tried to soothe the king. But Hamir's anger would not be appeased. Sullenly he rode back with Rano to Umarkot, and, as soon as they reached the city, flung him into prison. There Rano remained in a noisome cell for seven days and nights. On the eighth day his sister, the most beautiful of king Hamir's wives, begged the king to release her brother. At first Hamir refused; but at last he said, 'Tomorrow I will ask him a riddle. If he guesses it, he shall be a free man. If not, he shall go to the gallows.' It was in vain that Rano's sister tried to make the terms less hard.

Next morning Rano was led in chains to the royal palace. The king turned on him an evil look, and said, 'I have a riddle to ask you. If you guess it, you are a free man. If you fail to guess it you die this very day.' 'As the king pleases,' said Rano. 'Ask me the riddle that I may know my fate.' 'The riddle,' said king Hamir, 'is this :

'*How came the wide rent in the sari of silk?*'

Now Rano's wisdom had already been proved in his quest of Momul; so, after but a moment's hesitation, he answered:

'*The king toyed with his wife, whose child newly
born Cried to its mother to give it some milk :
She jumped to her feet, and her sari was torn.*'

Hamir was amazed at the ready wit of his vizier, and at once set him free and gave him back all, and more than all, his old honours; and every night, as before, Rano mounted his camel and rode to the princess's fairy palace.

At last, it fell out that Rano's wife and his father Kabir began to suspect Rano's intrigue. Rano's wife noticed red dust on her husband's clothes, whereas the dust of Umarkot was white. Rumours of Momul's love for Rano had spread over the country-side, and reached Kabir. He wondered how Rano could go to Momul's palace and return in one night, for it was two hundred miles from Umarkot. He went to Rano's stables and there learnt of the exceeding swiftness of Rano's she-camel. He at once ordered her to be taken out of the stables and killed. Then he had her buried in a distant pit.

That night, when Rano looked for his she-camel, he could not find her. Nor could he find his camel-men; for they had fled when Kabir led the she-camel away to kill her. At last he found a deaf camel-man, who had stayed behind. He bawled in his ears, 'Where is my she-camel?' The deaf man answered, 'Your father killed her; but she had a young camel, and it will carry you just as swiftly.' With these words he took Rano to the young camel's stable. They led it out, petted it, and promised it rich food if it carried Rano well. Then they bridled and saddled it; and it carried Rano even more swiftly than its mother had done. Thus he reached Momul's house at the appointed time.

But Rano did not spend all night with Momul as he had done before. Instead, he returned home early and, having cleaned his clothes, sought his wife's couch, so that she might not suspect him. So Rano's wife and his father thought that Rano no longer visited Momul.

Unhappily, the tale of Momul's love for Rano reached the ears of the queen, her mother, and of her sister Somal. The queen grieved for her daughter's good name; but Somal grieved because Momul no longer snared and robbed young men, that she might repay to king Nanda his lost treasure. Somal thought of a cruel trick. She went to Momul's palace and greeted her sister with feigned affection. Then she vowed that she must sleep with her on the same couch. When her sister had gone to sleep, Somal slipped from her side, and, exchanging her clothes for those of a man, again lay down by Momul's side.

In the meantime, Rano was speeding on his swift camel through the night to his beloved. As he went, he strayed some distance from the path, and meeting a camel-man, asked him the way to Momul's palace. Now the camel-man had been specially sent by Somal to wait for Rano, so he answered, 'Do you mean king Nanda's daughter, Momul, the mistress of Sital?' Then he showed Rano the way. Rano heard the lying words, but he thought no more of them, for he felt sure of Momul's love. He reached the palace, and, running upstairs, opened the door of Momul's room. By her side lay a young man asleep.

Rano's first impulse was to draw his sword and kill the guilty pair. But when he looked at Momul's sleeping face, he had not the heart to hurt her. So he put by her side his camel-switch, and then, going softly downstairs, mounted his camel, and rode back to Umarkot.

When Momul woke next morning, she saw by her side Rano's camel-switch. Going into the courtyard, she saw the tracks of his camel both coming and going. Then she guessed that Rano had come during the night, and seeing her in Somal's arms, had thought her faithless and had gone away. She sent him a message begging him to come back to her and telling him that the man whom he had seen sleeping, as he thought, at her side, was not a man at all, but her sister Somal. But Rano bade the messenger tell Momul that he could not disbelieve what he had himself seen, and that no woman would have worn a man's clothes. Momul sent a second messenger explaining the true facts, and many others afterwards. But Rano would not believe them; and at last he bade the messenger repeat to her these words: 'I will never forgive you, Momul, not though you come to my door as a beggar to ask my pardon.'

When the messenger gave Momul this message, she was at first overcome with grief; then she dressed herself like a sanyasi in a saffron robe, and, with a begging-bowl and a staff in her hands, went begging from village to village until she reached Umarkot. There she went to Rano's house and asked for alms. The young vizier did not pierce her disguise, but, being attracted by her face, asked, 'Whence have you come, holy sir? When did you become a sanyasi? Were you brought up in this holy state, or did you grow weary of the world and become the pupil of some saint?' 'Nay, fair youth,' replied the sanyasi, 'I am no man's pupil. I have learnt all the wisdom that man can teach, and I am myself a guru, so give me alms in the name of God.' Rano was greatly pleased by the reply, and bade the anchorite enter his house. Momul did so, and for many days she stayed with Rano as his honoured guest.

One day Rano challenged Momul to a game of dice, and asked her what the stakes should be. 'If I win,' said Momul, 'I shall stay with you always. If I lose, I go away tomorrow.' 'As you please,' answered Rano laughing; and the two sat down to the game. Rano made his throw, and Momul lifted her arm to make hers. Unhappily, in doing so, she bared her arm, and Rano saw on it a mole, which he had often noticed on Momul's arm. He rose and in a harsh voice bade her begone. She threw aside her saffron robe, hoping that he would melt at the sight of the form that he had once so often embraced. But he pushed her out of the house and into the street, and shut the door in her face.

Momul, broken-hearted, went out from the town, and hiring villagers to help her, built a great pyre in the plain. Then she mounted it and set fire to it with her own hands. The news that a suttee was burning herself outside the town reached Rano's ears, and he went to see. The sight of Momul about to die filled him with remorse, and he cried to her, 'Momul, come back to me. I was wrong. I believe you.' But Momul shook her head, and said, 'Dear one! now that you know I was true to you, I need no further happiness. You love me now; so let me die. Were I to live longer, you might again mistrust me.'

When she had spoken, the pyre fell inwards, and a great sheet of flame wrapped the princess round and consumed her. Then the memory of her beauty came back to Rano, and he felt that without Momul his life was worth nothing. Going close to the burning pyre, he sprang upon the spot where Momul had vanished in the flames. Thus in death the lovers were united.

READ MORE IN PENGUIN

In every corner of the world, on every subject under the sun, Penguin represents quality and variety – the very best in publishing today.

For complete information about books available from Penguin – including Puffins, Penguin Classics and Arkana – and how to order them, write to us at the appropriate address below. Please note that for copyright reasons the selection of books varies from country to country.

In India: Please write to *Penguin Books India Pvt Ltd, 706 Eros Apartments, 56 Nehru Place, New Delhi, 110019*

In the United Kingdom: Please write to *Dept. JC, Penguin Books Ltd, Bath Road, Harmondsworth, West Drayton, Middlesex, UB7 ODA, UK*

In the United States: Please write to *Penguin USA Inc., 375 Hudson Street, New York, NY 10014*

In Canada: Please write to *Penguin Books Canada Ltd, 10 Alcorn Avenue, Suite 300, Toronto, Ontario M4V 3B2*

In Australia: Please write to *Penguin Books Australia Ltd, 487 Maroondah Highway, Ring Wood, Victoria 3134*

In New Zealand: Please write to *Penguin Books (NZ) Ltd, 182–190 Wairau Road, Private Bag, Takapuna, Auckland 9*

In the Netherlands: Please write to *Penguin Books Netherlands B.V., Keizersgracht 231 NL–1016 DV Amsterdam*

In Germany : Please write to *Penguin Books Deutschland GmbH, Metzlerstrasse 26, 60595 Frankfurt am Main, Germany*

In Spain: Please write to *Penguin Books S. A., Bravo Murillo, 19-1' B, E-28015 Madrid, Spain*

In Italy: Please write to *Penguin Italia s.r.l., Via Felice Casati 20, I–20124 Milano*

In France: Please write to *Penguin France S. A., 17 rue Lejeune, F–31000 Toulouse*

In Japan: Please write to *Penguin Books Japan, Ishikiribashi Building, 2-5-4, Suido, Tokyo 112*

In Greece: Please write to *Penguin Hellas Ltd, Dimocritou 3, GR–106 71 Athens*

In South Africa: Please write to *Longman Penguin Southern Africa (Pty) Ltd, Private Bag X08, Bertsham 2013*

FOR THE BEST IN PAPERBACKS, LOOK FOR THE

THE GOLDEN WAIST CHAIN
Modern Hindi Short Stories
Edited by Sara Rai

A selection of some of the best Hindi stories of the last forty years, this collection is a representative volume of the *Nai Kahani* genre and includes the work of Nirmal Varma, Muktibodh and Mohan Rakesh among others. Sara Rai's translation skills couple with her heritage for she is Premchand's granddaughter.

Such collections would be welcome for fiction from other Indian languages as well

—*Makarand Paranjape in Femina*

THE PENGUIN BOOK OF MODERN INDIAN
SHORT STORIES
Edited by Stephen Alter & Wimal Dissanayake

This collection has eighteen stories by Bharati Mukherjee, Anita Dasai and Bhisham Sahni among others, some of them anthologized elsewhere to great acclaim. All of them have been written in the last fifty years and combined in a rich spectrum of pleasures that this popular genre has typically provided—especially in the hands of masters writing in over a dozen languages of the subcontinent.

As a glimpse into the nuts and bolts of the Indian middle class . . . the stories are invigorating vignettes.

—*Subhash K Jha*

Another myth that this selection succeeds in exploding is that Indian writing rests on a few giants like Tagore and Premchand. The reader needed to be introduced to 'modern' writing.

—*Financial Express.*